BIBLE
Trivia
CHALLENGE

BIBLE
Trivia
CHALLENGE

2001 Questions From
Genesis to Revelation

Conover Swofford
John Hudson Tiner

BARBOUR
PUBLISHING

Published by Barbour Publishing, Inc., P.O. Box 719, Uhrichsville, Ohio 44683 www.barbourbooks.com

Our mission is to publish and distribute inspirational products offering exceptional value and biblical encouragement to the masses.

 Member of the
Evangelical Christian
Publishers Association

Printed in the United States of America.

Contents

Welcome to
Bible Trivia Challenge

Are you ready to test your knowledge of the scripture? Here are 2,001 questions—covering every book of the Bible, from Genesis to Revelation—to see just how much you recall of God's Word.

Bible Trivia Challenge consists of two hundred ten-question quizzes, beginning with Creation, and moving, in biblical order, through The End of Time. You'll face open-ended questions, fill-in-the-blanks, multiple-choice queries, true/false statements, and more.

All questions are based on the King James Version of the Bible, but they should be clear to readers of more modern translations. Answers are provided beginning on page 325.

You'll enjoy flexing your memory muscles, learning some things you might never have known, and, as a bonus, perhaps seeing the flow of the biblical narrative in a new light. And be sure to stick around for the special 2,001st question following the final quiz—it'll put the whole book into a real-life perspective.

Welcome to *Bible Trivia Challenge*. Enjoy the journey ahead!

Quiz 1

Creation

*Like a master artist, God painted the universe
into existence in the first chapter of Genesis.
What do you remember about Creation?*

1. When did God create "the heaven and the earth"?

2. Fill in the blank: "And the earth was without _____, and void."

3. What is the Bible's first recorded word from God?

4. Which of the following was *not* marked by the "lights in the firmament of the heaven"?
    a) signs
    b) seasons
    c) days
    d) months

5. True or False: God called for sea creatures before He spoke the birds into existence.

6. Fill in the blanks: "God made the beast of the earth after his _____, and cattle after their ____"

7. How did God create man?
    a) "for our pleasure"

b) "with our blessing"
c) "to our glory"
d) "in our image"

8. What did God allow Adam and Eve to eat?
   a) seed-bearing herbs and fruit
   b) grasses
   c) birds
   d) fish

9. How many days of Creation were there?

10. How did God describe "every thing that he had made"?

Quiz 2

Adam, Eve, and Eden

According to the Bible, human beings quickly followed the creation of the universe. Here's a quiz on the first two people and their first home.

1. What did God use to form the first man?
   a) "the essence of heaven"
   b) "the dust of the ground"
   c) "the waters of Eden"
   d) "the fruit of the field"

2. Fill in the blanks: "[God] breathed into his nostrils the
_____ __ ____"

3. What word describes Adam and Eve's first home, Eden,
in Genesis 2:8?

4. What was Adam's job in Eden?
    a) "to enjoy it forever"
    b) "to build it for thy descendants"
    c) "to dress it and to keep it"
    d) "to protect it from harm"

5. True or False: The Nile was one of the four rivers of
Eden.

6. Fill in the blank: "The LORD God said, It is not good that
the man should be _____"

7. What did God have Adam do for all the animals?

8. What part of Adam did God use in forming his wife,
Eve?
    a) his heart
    b) a rib
    c) leg muscle
    d) hair

9. True or False: Adam gave his wife a name besides Eve.

10. How does Genesis 2:25 describe Adam and Eve, even
though they were "not ashamed"?

The Fall

*Give people a choice, and sometimes they'll
choose wrong. That's the story of Adam and Eve.
What do you recall of "the Fall"?*

1. Choose A or B: "Now the serpent was more A) evil B) subtle than any beast of the field which the Lord God had made."

2. After Adam and Eve ate the fruit, what happened to them first?

3. What did God call out to Adam after he and Eve had sinned in the Garden of Eden?

4. What did God tell the serpent?
   a) "thou art cursed above all cattle"
   b) "I will put enmity between thee and the woman"
   c) "upon thy belly shalt thou go"
   d) all of the above

5. True or False: God told the woman, "In sorrow thou shalt bring forth children."

6. Fill in the blank: "In the _____ of thy face shalt thou eat bread."

7. Adam called his wife's name Eve because she was
   a) the first woman created

b) Adam's helpmeet
c) created in the evening
d) the mother of all living

8. True or False: God made coats of skins to clothe Adam and Eve.

9. Choose A or B: God made Adam and Eve leave the Garden of Eden because A) they might eat of the tree of life and live forever B) they needed to be punished.

10. What did God place at the east of the garden to keep Adam and Eve out?

Quiz 4

Cain and Abel

Cain and Abel were born to Adam and Eve after the first couple sinned in the Garden of Eden. How much do you know about these two brothers?

1. True or False: Abel was a tiller of the ground and Cain was a keeper of sheep.

2. What did Cain bring as an offering to the Lord?

3. What did Abel bring as an offering to the Lord?

4. True or False: Cain was angry because God respected Abel's offering but not Cain's offering.

5. God said to Adam, "_____ lieth at the door."
    a) guilt
    b) sin
    c) death
    d) disappointment

6. Fill in the blank: "Cain rose up against Abel his brother, and _____ him."

7. When the Lord said to Cain, "Where is Abel thy brother?" what did Cain reply?

8. Choose A or B: When God cursed Cain, He told Cain that Cain would be A) "a fugitive and a vagabond" B) "hated by all."

9. Cain went to live in
    a) Nineveh
    b) Babel
    c) Nod
    d) Canaan

10. What was the name of the son Eve said God gave her to replace Abel?
    a) Methuselah
    b) Abraham
    c) Noah
    d) Seth

Quiz 5

Long Live the Ancients

*These people are known as antediluvians because
they lived before the great flood. What specifics
does the Bible record about them?*

1. How old was Adam when he died?
   - a) 969
   - b) 930
   - c) 905
   - d) 890

2. Seth's only son mentioned by name was
   - a) Jared
   - b) Mahalaleel
   - c) Enos
   - d) Cainan

3. Was Methusaleh Enoch's father or was Enoch Methusaleh's father?

4. What happened to Enoch?

5. Of these three people, who had the shortest lifespan?
   - a) Seth
   - b) Enoch
   - c) Methusaleh

6. Fill in the blank: Lamech begat _____.

7. Choose A or B: A) Lamech B) Noah lived 777 years.

8. How was Methusaleh related to Noah?
   a) Noah's grandfather
   b) Noah's great-grandfather
   c) Noah's great-great-grandfather
   d) Noah's great-great-great-grandfather

9. How old was Noah when his sons were born?
   a) 130
   b) 270
   c) 65
   d) 500

10. Name Noah's three sons.

Quiz 6

Noah and His Ark

Noah was known for his righteousness in a world filled with wickedness. Here's a quiz about him and his big boat.

1. After sin spread throughout the earth, God declared, "My _____ shall not always strive with man."
   a) spirit
   b) conscience

    c) patience

    d) love

2. Fill in the blank: "God saw that. . .the thoughts of his heart was only _____ continually."

3. True or False: The Lord repented that he had made man.

4. Fill in the blank: "Noah found _____ in the eyes of the Lord."

5. Fill in the blanks: "The earth. . .was _____ before God, and. . .was filled with _____."

6. The ark was made out of what kind of wood?

    a) cedar

    b) oak

    c) gopher

    d) mahogany

7. How many windows did the ark have?

8. How many stories did the ark have?

    a) 2

    b) 3

    c) 4

    d) 5

9. What reason did God give Noah for bringing two of every kind of animal into the ark?

10. Choose A or B: Noah did A) most B) all of what God commanded him.

Quiz 7

The Flood

Water, water, everywhere!
What do you recall about the great flood that
God sent in judgment of a sinful world?

1. The Lord told Noah to bring how many of each of the clean animals into the ark?
   a) three pairs
   b) one pair
   c) seven pairs
   d) ten pairs

2. How long did the Lord say He would make it rain?

3. Who were the eight people on the ark?

4. How did the animals go into the ark?

5. Choose A or B: A) Noah B) the Lord shut the door of the ark.

6. What type of bird did Noah send out first from the ark?

7. Fill in the blank: "The dove found no _____ for the sole of her foot."

8. When the dove returned to the ark the second time, it had what in its mouth?

    a) a seed
    b) a flower
    c) a worm
    d) an olive leaf

9. Fill in the blank: "Noah built an _____ unto the LORD."

10. God said in His heart after the flood was over, "I will not again _____ the ground."

    a) curse
    b) bless
    c) enrich
    d) water

Quiz 8

God's Promise to Noah

*God spared Noah and his family from the great flood.
What promises did God make to Noah
after the flood was over?*

1. Fill in the blanks: God blessed Noah and his sons and told them, "Be _____, and _____."

2. God told Noah after the flood, "The fear of you and the _____ of you shall be upon every beast of the earth."

3. Choose A or B: "Every moving thing that liveth shall be A) meat for B) sacred to you."

4. Fill in the blank: God told Noah He would establish a "covenant with you, and with your _____."

5. Choose A or B: God said, "I will A) remember B) honor my covenant."

6. What sign did God give Noah as a token of His covenant?

7. True or False: God promised Noah that the waters would "no more become a flood to destroy all flesh."

8. Fill in the blank: God said His covenant was _____.

9. Which of Noah's sons became the father of Canaan?

10. True or False: The whole world was overspread by the three sons of Noah.

Quiz 9

The Post-Flood World

*Several important events happened between the
flood and Abraham's time. These questions
show how God dealt with these generations.*

1. From which of Noah's three sons was Nimrod descended?

2. Choose A or B: Nimrod was a A) hunter B) giant.

3. The beginning of Nimrod's kingdom was
    a) Babel
    b) Canaan
    c) Nineveh
    d) Assyria

4. Fill in the blanks: "The whole earth was of one _____, and
    of one _____."

5. The people decided to build a tower whose top would reach
    where?

6. True or False: The Lord came down to see the tower.

7. God said about the people who were building the tower,
    "Nothing will be restrained from them, which they have
    _____ to do"?

8. True or False: The Lord confused their language and scattered them abroad.

9. What happened to the city?

10. What was this place called?
   a) Samaria
   b) Judah
   c) Babel
   d) Nineveh

Quiz 10

Abram and Sarai

Abram and Sarai were part of God's plan for world redemption. What do you remember about how He dealt with them?

1. God told Abram, "Get thee out of thy _____."

2. When the Lord blessed Abram, He said:
   a) "I will make of thee a great nation."
   b) "I will bless thee, and make thy name great."
   c) "I will bless them that bless thee."
   d) all of the above

3. Along with Sarai, what other family member did Abram take with him?

4. Fill in the blank: "They went. . .into the land of _____."

5. When Abram arrived in Canaan, there was a _____ in the land.
    a) king
    b) beast
    c) famine
    d) flood

6. Choose A or B: When Abram and Sarai went to Egypt, Abram told Sarai to say she was his A) sister B) cousin.

7. True or False: The Lord blessed Pharaoh because of Sarai.

8. The Lord changed Abram's name to Abraham because
    a) he would be exceeding fruitful
    b) he followed the Lord's commandments
    c) he was the friend of God
    d) God had made him the father of many nations

9. Fill in the blank: "Every man child among you shall be _____."

10. What did the Lord change Sarai's name to?

Quiz 11

Two Sons for Abraham

*The Bible gives some important details about
two of Abraham's sons, Ishmael and Isaac.
How much do you recall about them?*

1. Whose idea was it for Abram to have a child with Hagar?

2. True or False: Because Sarai dealt harshly with her, Hagar
   fled into the wilderness.

3. Who told Hagar, "Return to thy mistress"?

4. Who named Ishmael?
   a) the Lord
   b) Abram
   c) Hagar
   d) the angel of the Lord

5. What did Hagar call the name of the Lord who spoke to
   her?

6. What did Ishmael become?
   a) hunter
   b) archer
   c) farmer
   d) shepherd

7. How old was Abraham when Isaac was born?
   a) 100
   b) 75
   c) 125
   d) 230

8. Who said, "God hath made me to laugh"?

9. Fill in the blank: "The son of this bondwoman shall not be _____ with my son."

10. Choose A or B: Sending Ishmael away was A) grievous B) a relief to Abraham.

Quiz 12

Lot

Lot is not a plot of ground on which you build a house. This quiz is about a person who was related to Abraham.

1. Fill in the blanks: Abram was very rich in _____, _____, and _____.

2. Choose A or B: There was A) fellowship B) strife between Abram's and Lot's herdsmen.

3. Was it Abram or Lot who decided they should separate?

4. Fill in the blank: Lot chose the plain of _____.

5. Where did Abram dwell?

6. Fill in the blanks: "The men of Sodom were _____ and _____ before the Lord."

7. To whom did God make this promise, "All the land which thou seest, to thee will I give it"?
   a) Lot
   b) Abram
   c) Abraham's servant
   d) Sarah

8. Who was taken captive by the kings of Sodom?
   a) Abraham
   b) Sarah
   c) Melchizedek
   d) Lot

9. Fill in the blank: Melchizedek was a priest and king of _____.

10. True or False: Abram took goods from the King of Sodom on Lot's behalf.

Quiz 13

Sodom and Gomorrah

*You've probably heard plenty about Sodom and Gomorrah.
Here's a quiz that measures how much you remember
about the Bible's account of these two evil cities.*

1. Fill in the blank: The Lord said the sin of Sodom and
   Gomorrah was very _____.

2. True or False: Lot pleaded with the Lord not to destroy
   Sodom and Gomorrah if ten righteous people could be
   found there.

3. How many angels came to visit Lot?

4. Who said, "Where are the men which came in to thee this
   night?"

5. True or False: The men of Sodom tried to break down Lot's
   door.

6. Choose A or B: The angels at Lot's house struck the
   citizens of Sodom with A) blindness B) a plague.

7. When Lot told his sons-in-law what was happening, how
   did they respond?

8. The name of the city Lot escaped to was
    a) Jerusalem
    b) Zoar
    c) Jericho
    d) Babel

9. Lot's wife was turned into a pillar of salt because
    a) she refused to leave Sodom
    b) she insulted the angels
    c) she looked back at the destruction of the city
    d) she refused to obey Lot

10. Who were the only family members who escaped Sodom with Lot?

Quiz 14

Isaac

There's not much in the Bible about Abraham's son, Isaac. Just the facts, please, about this son of Abraham's old age.

1. When Sarah heard the Lord say she would have a son, how did she react?

2. True or False: God told Abraham to offer Esau as a burnt offering.

3. When Isaac asked Abraham where the lamb was for the offering, how did Abraham reply?

4. Fill in the blank: "Abraham stretched forth his hand, and took the knife to _____ his son."

5. Who stopped Abraham?

6. What was caught in the thicket?

7. When the angel of the Lord blessed Abraham, he said Abraham's seed would be as numerous as
   a) the inhabitants of Canaan
   b) the stars of heaven and the sands of the seashore
   c) the camels of the desert
   d) the birds of the sky

8. Whom did Abraham send to find a wife for Isaac?

9. Who gave Abraham's servant a drink of water and also drew water for his camels?
   a) Sarah
   b) Rachel
   c) Miriam
   d) Rebekah

10. True or False: Rebekah went willingly to be Isaac's wife.

Quiz 15

Jacob and Esau

These twin sons of Isaac quarreled like typical brothers.
What else do you know about them?

1. True or False: Isaac preferred Jacob, and Rebekah preferred Esau.

2. What did Esau give Jacob in return for a bowl of pottage?
    a) venison
    b) a coat of skins
    c) his birthright
    d) a bow and arrows

3. Whose idea was it for Jacob to steal Isaac's blessing from Esau?

4. Since Isaac's eyes were dim, how could he tell the difference between Jacob and Esau?

5. How did Jacob disguise himself to fool Isaac?

6. Why did Jacob have to flee to Rebekah's brother, Laban?

7. True or False: Isaac blessed Jacob and sent him on his way.

8. Choose A or B: When Jacob came to a certain place, he used stones to make A) an altar B) a pillow.

9. Fill in the blank: Jacob had a dream of a _____ reaching to heaven.

10. Jacob changed the name of the place from Luz to
    a) Bethel
    b) Bethlehem
    c) Bethany
    d) Jerusalem

Quiz 16

Jacob's Strange Family, Part 1

"Dysfunctional" well describes the family of the great patriarch Jacob. What do you remember about this rather nontraditional family?

1. Who was the first family member Jacob met when he came to Haran?

2. Fill in the blank: Jacob promised to work ____ years for Laban in order to marry Rachel.

3. When it came time to marry Rachel, how did Laban trick Jacob?

4. Choose A or B: The names of Rachel's and Leah's maids were A) Shiphrah and Puah B) Zilpah and Bilhah.

5. Of these children of Jacob, who was his firstborn?
    a) Gad
    b) Dan
    c) Levi
    d) Reuben

6. What was the name of Jacob's only daughter?

7. Who was the mother of Jacob's daughter?

8. Leah bore Jacob how many sons?
    a) two
    b) six
    c) three
    d) ten

9. What did Rachel steal from her father?

10. To whom was Laban referring when he said, "The LORD watch between me and thee, when we are absent one from another"?
    a) Esau
    b) Abraham's servant
    c) Jacob
    d) Isaac

Quiz 17

Jacob's Strange Family, Part 2

*It takes two quizzes to cover the crazy
family of Jacob. Now that's strange!*

1. Choose A or B: Jacob met a man, and they A) talked B)
   wrestled until the breaking of day.

2. True or False: When Jacob got ready to meet Esau, he put
   the maids and their sons first, Leah and her children
   second, and Rachel last.

3. Choose A or B: When Jacob met Esau, Esau was A)
   friendly B) unfriendly to Jacob.

4. Fill in the blank: "Jacob journeyed to Succoth, and built him
   an _____."

5. True or False: Shechem, a Hivite prince, wanted to marry
   Jacob's daughter.

6. Which two of Jacob's sons dealt with Shechem?
   a) Simeon and Levi
   b) Reuben and Judah
   c) Gad and Asher
   d) Dan and Issachar

7. Fill in the blank: Jacob took his family to Bethel and built an _____ there.

8. What did God change Jacob's name to?

9. What was Rachel's original name for Benjamin?
   a) Benoni
   b) Ben-jaakan
   c) Ben-arbi
   d) Ben-hur

10. True or False: Rachel had other sons after she gave birth to Benjamin.

Quiz 18

Joseph

Joseph was a good boy who wound up first in a bad place, then later in a good place. See how much you recall about his interesting life.

1. Fill in the blank: "Israel _____ Joseph more than all his children."

2. Choose A or B: Israel made Joseph a coat of A) many skins B) many colors.

3. How old was Joseph when he dreamed his first dream?

4. Joseph's first dream was about
    a) sand on the sea shore
    b) sheep
    c) sheaves of wheat
    d) cattle

5. Choose A or B: In Joseph's second dream, the sun, moon, and stars A) spoke B) bowed to him.

6. When Joseph told his family about his second dream, who rebuked him?

7. Fill in the blanks: When Joseph went to check on his brothers, they stripped him of his _____ and threw him into a _____ .

8. Joseph was taken to what country after he was sold into slavery by his brothers?
    a) Assyria
    b) Egypt
    c) Persia
    d) Greece

9. True or False: Joseph was thrown into prison in Egypt because he refused to interpret Pharaoh's dream.

10. When Joseph interpreted the dreams of the butler and the baker, what did he predict would happen to the butler?
    a) he would be executed by Pharaoh
    b) he would be sold into slavery
    c) he would remain in prison for five more years
    d) he would be restored to his job

Pharaoh's Dreams

*The king of Egypt had some bad dreams, and it took
an imprisoned Hebrew slave to sort them out for him.
Answer all the questions in this quiz correctly,
and you're a winner like Joseph was.*

1. How many years was Joseph in prison before Pharaoh had
   his dreams?
   a) five
   b) two
   c) seven
   d) ten

2. Fill in the blank: In Pharaoh's first dream, seven ill-favored
   and lean kine _____ seven well-favored and fat kine.

3. What was Pharaoh's second dream about?

4. True or False: Pharaoh sent for the wise men and magicians
   of Egypt to interpret his dreams.

5. Who told Pharaoh about Joseph?

6. What was the interpretation of both dreams?

7. Choose A or B: Joseph told Pharaoh to choose a man A)
   "noble and rich" B) "discreet and wise" and set him over the
   land of Egypt.

8. Fill in the blank: Pharaoh took off his _____ and gave it to Joseph.

9. Fill in the blank: Pharaoh made Joseph _____ over all the land of Egypt.

10. Pharaoh named Joseph to a high position in the Egyptian government that charged him with
   a) storing food
   b) ruling over the slaves
   c) building the pyramids
   d) serving as Pharaoh's bodyguard

Quiz 20

Israel in Egypt

*The members of Jacob's family took a journey into Egypt.
How long did they stay, and what happened to them there?
This quiz should jog your memory.*

1. Why did Jacob send his sons to Egypt?

2. Jacob wouldn't let Benjamin go to Egypt with his brothers because
   a) he was Jacob's favorite
   b) he was too young

c) he didn't want to go

d) mischief, or trouble, might befall him

3. Fill in the blank: Joseph was the _____ over the land of Egypt.

4. True or False: When Joseph's brothers came to Egypt, he didn't know who they were but they recognized him.

5. Fill in the blank: Joseph accused his brothers of being _____.

6. When his brothers brought Benjamin to Egypt on their second trip, what did Joseph put in Benjamin's sack?

a) a robe

b) a pair of sandals

c) a crown

d) a silver cup

7. Which of Joseph's brothers offered to be Joseph's servant if Joseph would release Benjamin?

8. True or False: When Joseph made himself known to his brothers, he wept.

9. Who said, "Ye thought evil against me; but God meant it unto good"?

10. Fill in the blank: "There arose up a new king over Egypt, which knew not _____."

Quiz 21

Moses

Moses was God's hand-picked man for a big task.
See if you recall how Moses geared up for this assignment.

1. Why did Moses' mother put Moses in the ark in the river?

2. Who watched over Moses in the river?

3. Choose A or B: Pharaoh's A) wife B) daughter found
   Moses.

4. True or False: Moses' sister was allowed to nurse him.

5. Moses was named Moses because
   a) he was drawn out of the water
   b) it was a family name
   c) he was a Hebrew child
   d) God named him that

6. Why did Moses have to flee from Egypt?
   a) he ran out of money
   b) he killed an Egyptian man
   c) he led a rebellion against Pharaoh
   d) he went to search for his father

7. Fill in the blank: The priest of Midian had _____ daughters.

8. When God spoke to Moses from the burning bush, what two signs did God give Moses to use so the people would believe him?

9. Who went with Moses to talk to Pharaoh?
   a) his sister
   b) the elders of Israel
   c) his brother Aaron
   d) his mother

10. True or False: Pharaoh said, "Who is the LORD, that I should obey his voice?"

Quiz 22

The Plagues, Part 1

Nobody likes to be plagued, but the Egyptians brought it on themselves because of Pharaoh's stubbornness. How much do you know about the first five plagues?

1. True or False: When Aaron's rod became a serpent, the Egyptian magicians also made their rods become serpents.

2. Fill in the blank: Aaron's rod _____ the Egyptian magicians' rods.

3. Fill in the blanks: The first plague was _____ turned to
_____.

4. True or False: When God brought frogs on the land, the
Egyptian magicians produced snakes to gobble up the frogs.

5. The Egyptian magicians told Pharaoh that the plague of
lice was
   a) the finger of God
   b) something they could duplicate
   c) nothing they should worry about
   d) a freak happening that would soon disappear

6. Fill in the blank: When God sent the swarms of flies upon
Egypt, the flies were everywhere except in the land of _____.

7. Fill in the blank: Every time Pharaoh refused to let the
Israelites go, he _____ his heart.

8. God told Moses to say to Pharaoh, "Let my people go, that
they may _____ me."
   a) approach
   b) seek
   c) worship
   d) serve

9. Fill in the blank: "There shall nothing ____ of all that is the
children's of Israel."

10. Choose A or B: The fifth plague was against the
Egyptians' A) wheat B) cattle.

The Plagues, Part 2

*The Egyptians had so many plagues,
it takes two quizzes to cover them all. Let's see how
well you wrap them up with these questions.*

1. What did God tell Moses to sprinkle in the sight of
   Pharaoh?
   a) ashes
   b) sand
   c) blood
   d) water

2. True or False: The magicians couldn't stand before Moses
   because they were struck with boils, or sores.

3. True or False: The Lord softened Pharaoh's heart.

4. Choose A or B: In order to start the plague of fire and hail,
   the Lord told Moses to A) stretch his rod toward heaven B)
   speak the word.

5. True or False: The hail broke every tree of the field.

6. Who said, "I have sinned this time" and "the Lord is
   righteous"?

7. Fill in the blank: After the fire and hail came the plague of
   _____.

8. True or False: The plague in Question 7 covered the earth
   but did not cause any significant damage in Egypt.

9. The plague of darkness lasted how many days?
   a) five
   b) four
   c) three
   d) two

10. What was the last plague against Egypt?

Quiz 24

The Passover

Passover is not something a bird or airplane does.
How much do you know about this
important Israelite celebration?

1. Choose A or B: The lamb of the first Passover was to be A)
   male B) female.

2. Fill in the blank: The lamb of Question 1 was to be without
   _____.

3. The lamb was to be killed on what day of the month?
    a) first
    b) tenth
    c) fourteenth
    d) thirtieth

4. True or False: The blood of the lamb was to be put on the two side posts and the upper door of each house.

5. Fill in the blanks: The Israelites were to eat the roasted lamb with _____ bread and _____ herbs.

6. True or False: The Israelites were to eat with shoes on their feet and their staffs in their hands.

7. Why was this event called Passover?

8. Choose A or B: "And this day shall be unto you for a A) memorial B) sacrifice."

9. True or False: The feast was to last nine days.

10. What type of plant was to be dipped in the blood to put the blood on the doorposts?
    a) hazel
    b) hyssop
    c) hickory
    d) grass

Quiz 25

The Exodus

The Exodus was one of the most important events in Israel's history. Find out why by answering these questions.

1. What did the Israelites borrow from the Egyptians?

2. How many years had the Israelites been in Egypt?
    a) 132
    b) 275
    c) 311
    d) 430

3. Fill in the blank: The Lord told Moses to _____ all the firstborn.

4. When the Israelites left Egypt, why did God keep them from going through the land of the Philistines?
    a) It was full of giants.
    b) It was too far away.
    c) It was at war.
    d) It was hard to find.

5. Whose bones did Moses take when the Israelites left Egypt?

6. Fill in the blanks: "The Lord went before them by day in a pillar of a _____...and by night in a pillar of _____."

7. What did Moses stretch over the sea to divide the waters?

8. Fill in the blank: "The children of Israel went into the midst of the sea upon the _____ ground."

9. How did the Lord trouble the hosts of Egypt?
    a) He took off their chariot wheels.
    b) He caused their horses to founder.
    c) He made them fall out of their chariots.
    d) He struck them blind.

10. Fill in the blank: The waters returned and covered the hosts of Pharaoh and there remained "not so much as ___ of them."

Quiz 26

Miracle Food and Drink

God kept His people alive by providing them with food and water in the wilderness. Here's a quiz to see how much you recall about His provision.

1. Fill in the blank: The Lord said, "I will rain _____ from heaven."

2. True or False: The Israelites had to gather three times as much manna the day before the Sabbath.

3. What type of birds did the Lord send for the Israelites to eat?
   a) chickens
   b) dove
   c) quail
   d) geese

4. What happened to the manna if the Israelites left it overnight?

5. Choose A or B: The A) Lord B) people called this mysterious food Manna.

6. Fill in the blank: "The people _____ on the seventh day."

7. What was the name of the wilderness where the Israelites were camping?
   a) Gaza
   b) Sinai
   c) Sin
   d) Tribulation

8. Why did the Israelites complain against Moses?

9. True or False: Moses got water from a rock by striking the rock.

10. True or False: Moses called the name of the place Bethel and Berothah.

The Ten Commandments

This quiz has a lot of "thou shalts" and "thou shalt nots."
See how many of them you can sort out.

1. Fill in the blanks: "Thou shalt have ____ ____ ____ before me."

2. "Thou shalt not make unto thee any _____ _____."
   a) false weights
   b) stone tablets
   c) graven image
   d) strong wine

3. Choose A or B: Thou shalt not bow down or serve other gods because A) the Lord is a jealous God B) a plague will come upon you.

4. Fill in the blank: "The Lord will not hold him guiltless that taketh his name ____ ____."

5. Fill in the blank: "_____ the sabbath day, to keep it holy."

6. True or False: "Honour thy father and thy mother: that thy days may be long upon the land."

7. Fill in the blank: Quote the next commandment after

"Honour thy father and thy mother." "Thou shalt not
_____."

8. Fill in the blank: "Thou shalt not commit _____."

9. Fill in the blanks: "Thou shalt not bear _____ _____
against thy neighbour."

10. "Thou shalt not covet thy neighbour's. . ."
   a) "house"
   b) "wife"
   c) "manservant"
   d) all of the above

Quiz 28

The Ark of the Covenant

*The ark of the covenant was one of Israel's most
sacred objects. Separate fact from fiction by
answering the questions in this quiz.*

1. The ark was made of what kind of wood?
   a) gopher
   b) mahogany
   c) shittim
   d) ebony

2. True or False: The ark's dimensions were two and a half cubits long, two and a half cubits wide and one and a half cubits high.

3. Fill in the blank: The ark was overlaid with pure _____.

4. Why were the four rings on the ark, one on each corner?

5. What was the name for the top of the ark?

6. Choose A or B: The two figures on top of the ark were A) seraphim B) cherubim.

7. Choose A or B: The part of the figures that touched above the top of the ark were their A) arms B) wings.

8. True or False: The Lord would meet and commune with His people from between the two figures on the top of the ark.

9. What was put into the ark?

10. What tribe was set aside to be the bearers of the ark?
    a) Judah
    b) Reuben
    c) Levi
    d) Dan

Quiz 29

The Tabernacle

God directed His people to build the tabernacle as a place of worship. These questions should impress you with how much it differed from modern houses of worship.

1. How many curtains did the Tabernacle have?

2. The curtains contained which of the following colors?
   a) blue
   b) purple
   c) scarlet
   d) all of the above

3. Fill in the blank: "And the _____ shall divide unto you between the holy place and the most holy."

4. What was put in the most holy place?

5. Choose A or B: The four corners of the altar had A) rings B) horns.

6. Fill in the blank: The altar was overlaid with _____.

7. True or False: The oil for the lamp was to be pure whale oil.

8. The breastplate for the priest contained how many stones?
   a) twelve
   b) three
   c) six
   d) nine

9. True or False: The gold plate for the priest's breastplate was engraved with the words HOLINESS TO THE LORD.

10. Who did God choose as the master craftsman who would build the tabernacle?
    a) Hiram
    b) Bezaleel
    c) Aaron
    d) Joab

Quiz 30

Golden Trouble

*Idolatry raises its ugly head in these questions.
Find out what happened and how God
responded to false worship among His people.*

1. Choose A or B: The people asked Aaron to make them a god because A) they were bored B) Moses was away a long time.

2. Where was Moses at this time?

3. What did Aaron ask the people to give him?

4. Who actually made the golden calf?

5. Fill in the blank: "Get thee down," God told Moses, "for thy people. . .have _____ themselves."

6. Choose A or B: The sight of the people worshipping the golden calf caused Moses to A) yell at them B) break the stone tables.

7. True or False: Moses ground the golden calf into powder, mixed it with water, and forced the Israelites to drink it.

8. Choose A or B: What did Aaron tell Moses about how the golden calf was made? A) The people made it B) Aaron cast the gold into the fire and it came out a calf.

9. When Moses said, "Who is on the Lord's side?" all the sons of which tribe joined him?
    a) Judah
    b) Benjamin
    c) Levi
    d) Gad

10. How many people were killed that day?
    a) one thousand
    b) two thousand
    c) three thousand
    d) five thousand

Laws of Leviticus

*Laws and Leviticus go together like pencil and paper.
You're a genius if you can identify all these laws
and practices from Old Testament times!*

1. Fill in the blank: The offering to make atonement was called
   a _____ offering.

2. Which of the following was *not* an offering?
   a) sin offering
   b) peace offering
   c) trespass offering
   d) priest offering

3. Choose A or B: "Ye shall eat no manner of A) blood B) fat,
   of ox, or of sheep, or of goat."

4. With what were the priests anointed?

5. True or False: Samuel and Eli were devoured by fire
   because they offered strange fire to the Lord.

6. Fill in the blank: The foods the Israelites were forbidden to
   eat were _____ to them.

7. Which of the following foods were the Israelites not
   allowed to eat?
   a) locusts
   b) beetles

c) grasshoppers

d) hares

8. If a person had a skin plague, he was required to show it to whom?

9. A person with a skin plague was shut away for how many days?

a) three

b) five

c) seven

d) fourteen

10. True or False: The priest had to declare garments that had leprosy clean or unclean.

Quiz 32

More Laws of Leviticus

As if one quiz on laws and Leviticus were not enough, here's another to test your patience and stamina.

1. Who could pronounce a leper clean?

2. True or False: As part of their cleansing, lepers had to shave off all their hair, beard, and eyebrows.

3. The offerings for lepers being cleansed were
    a) sin offerings
    b) trespass offerings
    c) burnt offerings
    d) all of the above

4. True or False: If leprosy contaminated a house, it was torn down immediately.

5. Fill in the blank: On the Day of Atonement, there were two goats—one for the Lord and the other for the _____.

6. Choose A or B: A peace offering was to be eaten A) on the day it was offered B) only by the priest.

7. Fill in the blank: "Sanctify yourselves. . .and be ye _____: for I am the Lord your God."

8. True or False: The priests were not to be defiled for the dead among their people.

9. What happened if a blemished animal was offered for a sacrifice?

10. Who were the only people allowed to eat the shewbread in the Tabernacle?
    a) kings and their wives
    b) Aaron and his sons
    c) warriors and their families
    d) Abraham and Sarah

Quiz 33

Celebrations

*Everybody likes a holiday and the celebration that goes
along with it. How many of these special occasions
among the Israelites can you identify?*

1. Fill in the blank: The Lord called His feasts holy _____.

2. Fill in the blank: The Sabbath was to be a day of _____.

3. The fourteenth day of the first month was
     a) the Feast of Booths
     b) First Gathering
     c) Passover
     d) Jubilee

4. Choose A or B: During the Passover the Israelites were to
   do no servile work on A) the first and seventh days B) all
   the days.

5. Fill in the blank: During the Feast of Firstfruits, the priest
   was to wave a _____ before the Lord.

6. True or False: The Israelites could eat neither bread,
   parched corn (grain), or green corn (grain) until they had
   brought their offering of firstfruits to the Lord.

7. What was gleaning?

8. True or False: The Day of Atonement was celebrated on the tenth day of the tenth month.

9. The Feast of Tabernacles celebration lasted how many days?
   a) three
   b) seven
   c) ten
   d) fourteen

10. The Feast of Booths celebration lasted how many days?
   a) two
   b) three
   c) five
   d) seven

Quiz 34

Exploring Canaan

Moses wanted to know what the Israelites were up against before they entered the land. Here's a quiz about the exploratory journey and what they discovered.

1. Fill in the blanks: "Send thou men, that they may _____ the _____ of Canaan."

2. How many men were sent to explore the land?

3. Choose A or B: Moses sent the men A) to the river Jordan B) up into a mountain to see the land.

4. Moses told the spies to see
   a) whether the land was good or bad
   b) whether the people were strong or weak
   c) whether the people lived in tents or strong holds
   d) all of the above

5. Choose A or B: The spies went into the land of Canaan from the A) north B) south.

6. True or False: They found coconuts so large that it took two men to carry three or four in a basket.

7. How many days were the spies gone?
   a) ten
   b) twenty
   c) thirty
   d) forty

8. Fill in the blanks: The spies said the land flowed with _____ and _____.

9. Who quieted the people before Moses and challenged them to take the land immediately?

10. How did the people respond to this challenge?

Quiz 35

Rebellion

Things didn't always go smoothly for Moses as he led the people. These questions show the dark side of the journey of the Israelites toward the Promised Land.

1. Fill in the blank: "When the people complained, it _____ the Lord."

2. Who said, "I am not able to bear all this people alone"?
      a) Moses
      b) Aaron
      c) God
      d) Miriam

3. What happened when the people got greedy eating the quail?

4. Miriam and Aaron spoke against Moses because
      a) they were jealous of his authority
      b) he was a weak leader
      c) he married an Ethiopian woman
      d) he had sinned against the Lord

5. True or False: Because Miriam spoke against Moses, she had leprosy for seven days.

6. When the Israelites threatened to return to Egypt, who said, "If the Lord delight in us, then he will bring us into this land"?

7. Because of their complaining, what punishment did the Lord pronounce on Israel?

8. How many years was their punishment to last?

9. What two men were the exception to the Lord's pronouncement of punishment?

10. True or False: When Moses told the people about the Lord's pronouncement of punishment, they mourned greatly.

Quiz 36

Wilderness Wanderings

Here are some questions about the Israelites' experience of wandering in the wilderness. How much do you remember about these dreary years, as described in the book of Numbers?

1. What did the Lord tell Moses to have the Israelites put on their clothes to help them remember His commandments?
   a) precious stones
   b) stripes
   c) fringes
   d) belts

2. How many princes of the assembly did Korah lead against Moses?

3. Who said, "Even to morrow the Lord will shew who are his"?

4. True or False: The Lord caused a great flood that swept Korah away.

5. Choose A or B: How did the Lord show that Aaron was His choice? A) He caused Aaron's rod to blossom. B) He caused a flame of fire to appear over Aaron's head.

6. True or False: The Lord told Moses to speak to the rock and water would come forth.

7. Why did the Lord tell Moses that Moses wouldn't bring the Israelites into the Promised Land?

8. When Aaron died, he was buried on Mount
   a) Sinai
   b) Moriah
   c) Horeb
   d) Hor

9. What did the Lord send to punish the people when they complained against Moses and the Lord?
   a) stinging scorpions
   b) fierce lions
   c) biting insects
   d) fiery serpents

10. Fill in the blank: Moses placed a brass _____ on a pole and held it up for the people to see and be saved.

Quiz 37

Balaam and Balak

Balaam and Balak were not twin brothers, but they were definitely a strange pair. These questions based on the book of Numbers tell you all about their working relationship.

1. True or False: King Balak thought he could get Balaam to curse the Israelites.

2. Balak sent the elders from where to Balaam?
   a) Moab
   b) Midian
   c) Meribah
   d) a and b

3. Who said to Balaam, "Thou shalt not go with them"?
   a) an angel
   b) God
   c) Balaam's friends
   d) Balaam's wife

4. Who did Balak send to Balaam after he refused the request of Balak's first messengers?

5. Choose A or B: Balak promised Balaam A) great honor B) riches if Balaam would come help him.

6. True or False: The second time Balak's representatives came, the Lord told Balaam to go with them.

7. The animal on which Balaam was riding stopped because it saw what?
- a) a lion blocking the way
- b) a nest of hornets
- c) the angel of the Lord
- d) a blinding light

8. True or False: Balaam's camel spoke to him.

9. How many times did Balaam bless the Israelites?

10. True or False: King Balak was happy with Balaam.

Quiz 38

The Parting Words of Moses, Part 1

Moses had a lot to say to the Israelites in the book of Deuteronomy as he drew near the end of his days. What advice did he give them?

1. Choose A or B: "Behold, ye are this day as A) the stars of heaven B) the sand on the sea shore for multitude."

2. Because Moses couldn't bear the burden of the people by himself, he did what?

70

3. True or False: The people declared that the Lord hated them.

4. The Lord told Moses not to disturb the Moabites because the Lord had given their land to the children of
    a) Esau
    b) Ishmael
    c) Lot
    d) Seth

5. Fill in the blank: "The Lord our God delivered into our hands _____ . . .the king of Bashan."

6. The Lord brought the Israelites out of Egypt because
    a) He loved their fathers
    b) they were a worthy and obedient people
    c) they deserved it
    d) the Egyptians grew weary of them

7. Fill in the blank: "Hear, O Israel: The Lord our God is ____ Lord."

8. Fill in the blank: "Ye shall not go after other _____."

9. Choose A or B: "It shall be our A) duty B) righteousness, if we observe to do all these commandments before the Lord our God."

10. Fill in the blank: "The Lord thy God shall bring thee into the land whither thou goest to _____ it."

Quiz 39

The Parting Words of Moses, Part 2

*In this quiz Moses continues his long speeches
to the Israelites in the book of Deuteronomy.
How well do you think he held their attention?*

1. What does the Lord require of us?
   - a) to walk in all His ways
   - b) to love Him
   - c) to serve Him
   - d) all of the above

2. Fill in the blank: "Ye shall _____ destroy all the places,
   wherein the nations. . .served their gods."

3. Fill in the blank: "Ye shall not eat the _____; ye shall pour it
   upon the earth as water."

4. How were the people to treat a false prophet?
   - a) show him kindness and respect
   - b) cast him out of the camp
   - c) put him to death
   - d) charge him with blasphemy before the elders

5. Which of the following could the Israelites eat?
   - a) camel   c) eagle
   - b) swine   d) roebuck

6. True or False: The Israelites were supposed to tithe the increase of their seed.

7. Fill in the blank: Every seven years every creditor that lendeth to his neighbor shall _____ it.

8. A Hebrew slave was to serve how many years before being set free?
    a) six   c) twelve
    b) three   d) fifteen

9. Choose A or B: The judges and officers were in all the A) gates B) cities.

10. True or False: A person who killed another person could flee to a city of refuge.

Quiz 40

Moses' End

Moses is such an important person in the Bible that he stretches across four books: Exodus, Leviticus, Numbers, and Deuteronomy. But these questions are all about his final days as described in Deuteronomy.

1. How old was Moses when he died?
    a) 75 years old   c) 175 years old
    b) 120 years old   d) 196 years old

2. True or False: The Lord told Moses that Moses would not go over the Jordan.

3. Fill in the blank: Moses chose _____ to lead the Israelites.

4. When Moses wrote the law, to whom did he deliver it?

5. Fill in the blank: "The LORD appeared in the tabernacle in a pillar of a _____."

6. Who said, "Behold, thou shalt sleep with thy fathers"?

7. Choose A or B: Moses went up from the plains to the mountain of A) Nebo B) Sinai.

8. What did the Lord show Moses from the top of the mountain?
      a) a herd of grazing camels
      b) the camps of the Canaanites
      c) the well-traveled roads of Moab
      d) all the land He had promised the Israelites

9. How many days did the Israelites mourn Moses?
      a) seven
      b) fourteen
      c) thirty
      d) sixty

10. Fill in the blanks: "And there arose not a prophet since in Israel like unto Moses, whom the Lord knew _____ to _____."

Quiz 41

Say Hello to Joshua

*Joshua faced the daunting task of
fillingthe shoes of the great leader, Moses.
Complete this quiz to see how he measured up.*

1. Fill in the blank: "Joshua. . .was full of the spirit of _____."

2. When the Lord spoke to Joshua after Moses died, what did
   He tell Joshua to do?
   a) get ready to return to Egypt
   b) cross the Jordan River and enter the Promised Land
   c) wander in the wilderness for forty years
   d) send spies into the region of Moab

3. Fill in the blank: "Every place that the sole of your foot shall
   tread upon, that have I _____ unto you."

4. True or False: The Lord told Joshua to divide the land.

5. What did the Lord tell Joshua would make Joshua have
   good success?

6. Fill in the blank: "Be _____ and of a good _____; be not
   afraid."

7. Choose A or B: Joshua commanded the A) elders B)
   officers of the people to tell the people to prepare to cross
   the Jordan River.

8. Joshua told the people they would pass over the Jordan River in how many days?
   a) seven
   b) ten
   c) three
   d) two

9. True or False: The Reubenites, the Gadites, and half the tribe of Manasseh were to cross the Jordan River before their brethren.

10. What did the people promise Joshua they would do?
   a) mourn for Moses for forty days
   b) camp by the Jordan River until the weather changed
   c) wait for further instructions from the Lord
   d) listen to Joshua as they had listened to Moses

Quiz 42

Crossing Jordan

God gave the Israelites some specific instructions about crossing the Jordan River into the Promised Land. Judge how they followed His commands by completing this quiz.

1. How many men did Joshua send out to spy secretly?

2. Whose house did the spies come to?
   a) Rachel's
   b) Miriam's
   c) Rahab's
   d) Rebekah's

3. Choose A or B: The spies told the woman to hang a A) rope B) scarlet thread out of her window.

4. True or False: The spies told Joshua that "the inhabitants of the country do faint because of us."

5. What did the priests take up and carry before the people?
   a) the ark of the covenant
   b) two stone tablets
   c) Aaron's rod
   d) the bones of Moses

6. How many men were selected from each tribe to participate in carrying the ark across the Jordan River?

7. True or False: When the priests stepped into the Jordan River, the waters stopped flowing.

8. Fill in the blank: "Take. . .out of the midst of _____ . . . twelve stones."

9. The stones were to be a sign of what?

10. True or False: The priests waited until all the people had crossed the river, then they waded across.

Jericho

Jericho was a heavily fortified Canaanite city. How did God deliver it into the hands of the Israelites?

1. What did Joshua see when he stood before the city of Jericho?
   a) a pillar of cloud
   b) the captain of the host of the Lord
   c) a vision of Moses
   d) a massive army of Edomites

2. True or False: The city of Jericho was shut up so no one could go in or out.

3. Fill in the blanks: "See, I have _____ into thine _____ Jericho."

4. Fill in the blank: For six days, the Israelites were to march _____ around Jericho.

5. How many priests were to bear trumpets before the ark?
   a) seven
   b) ten
   c) twelve
   d) fifty

6. When the priests blew the trumpets, what were the Israelites to do?

7. Fill in the blank: The wall of the city shall fall down _____.

8. True or False: On the seventh day, the Israelites marched around Jericho seven times.

9. Fill in the blank: The only people saved in Jericho were _____ and her family.

10. True or False: The spoils taken from the city of Jericho were distributed among the people.

Quiz 44

Stealing Trouble

Trouble has a way of cropping up when things are going great. This quiz shows the troublesome thing that happened after the Israelites captured the city of Jericho.

1. Who took the accursed thing?
    a) Achan
    b) Reuben
    c) Caleb
    d) Eleazar

2. Who said, "Go up and view the country"?

3. Choose A or B: A) Three thousand B) thirty thousand Israelites went up to take the city of Ai.

4. Fill in the blank: "The men of Ai. . ._____ them from before the gate even unto Shebarim."

5. When Joshua heard the news, he
   a) cried out
   b) rent his clothes
   c) fell on his face
   d) b and c

6. How did Joshua find out who took the accursed thing?

7. True or False: The accursed thing consisted of a garment, as well as silver and gold.

8. Choose A or B: The accursed thing was found buried A) outside the man's tent B) in the middle of the man's tent.

9. Who said, "The Lord shall trouble thee this day"?

10. What happened to the man who took the accursed thing?
    a) he was rewarded for his bravery
    b) he was reprimanded by Joshua
    c) he was imprisoned for thirty days
    d) he was stoned and burned

Quiz 45

Battling For Canaan

*Canaan didn't just fall into the hands of the Israelites
without a fight. Complete this quiz to see how God
led the people in the conquest of the land.*

1. What strategy did the Israelites use against Ai?

2. True or False: The Israelites never succeeded in conquering
   the city of Ai.

3. What did Joshua build on Mount Ebal?

4. True or False: The Gibeonites tricked Joshua into not doing
   battle with them.

5. True or False: The Gibeonites became bondservants to the
   Israelites.

6. What nation or tribal group was Joshua fighting when the
   Lord made the sun stand still?
   a) the Edomites
   b) the Amorites
   c) the Hittites
   d) the Egyptians

7. Fill in the blank: "[Joshua] left none remaining, but
   _____ destroyed all that breathed, as the Lord God of
   Israel commanded."

8. True or False: The king of Hazor joined with the kings of Madon, Shimron, and Achshaph to fight against the Israelites.

9. According to Joshua 12:24, how many kings were defeated by Joshua's forces?
    a) twenty-one
    b) thirty-one
    c) forty-one
    d) fifty-one

10. Fill in the blank: "There remaineth yet very much land to be _____."

Quiz 46

Here Come the Judges

The judges in the book of Judges didn't wear black robes and swing gavels. These questions should help you sort out who they were and what they did.

1. True or False: The Lord raised up judges to deliver the Israelites from their enemies.

2. Choose A or B: Othniel, the first judge of Israel, was the son of A) Joshua's B) Caleb's brother.

3. Choose A or B: Ehud went against Eglon, the king of A) Moab B) Edom.

4. True or False: Shamgar killed six hundred Philistines with a spear.

5. The person who campaigned to make himself a judge was
   a) Abimelech
   b) Tola
   c) Jair
   d) Jephthah

6. True or False: Abimelech was the son of Gideon, also known as Jerubbaal. (NLT)

7. Jephthah made a vow to the Lord that he would sacrifice
   a) forty bullocks
   b) an unblemished ram
   c) the first thing that came out of his house to meet him
   d) a pair of turtledoves

8. Choose A or B: Ibzan was from A) Bethlehem B) Jerusalem.

9. True or False: Abdon had fifteen sons.

10. Fill in the blank: After each judge died, the children of Israel did _____ in the sight of the Lord.

A Mighty Strong Woman

Deborah, a female judge, is one of the most interesting women in the Bible. Answer these questions to determine how she led her people to victory.

1. Jabin was the king of
    a) Canaan
    b) the Philistines
    c) Ammon
    d) Edom

2. True or False: Jabin was the captain of Sisera's army.

3. Fill in the blanks: Deborah dwelt under a _____ _____.

4. True or False: Barak told Deborah he would go fight only if she went with him.

5. Fill in the blank: Deborah told Barak that the Lord would sell Sisera into the hand of _____ _____.

6. Heber was a
    a) Kenite
    b) Moabite
    c) Edomite
    d) Philistine

7. True or False: Sisera fled to the tent of Heber and Heber's wife, Jael, because there was peace between Jabin and Heber.

8. How did Jael welcome Sisera when he arrived at her tent?

9. True or False: Jael killed Sisera by suffocating him with a pillow while he was asleep.

10. Who said, "Praise ye the LORD for the avenging of Israel"?

Quiz 48

Gideon

*Gideon got off to a slow start, but he ended well.
How did God use him to rout the enemies of His people?*

1. True or False: Because of the Midianites, the Israelites had to live in caves and strong holds.

2. Choose A or B: The Midianites seemed like
   A) grasshoppers B) ants because of their great number.

3. When the angel of the Lord appeared to Gideon, he was
   a) threshing wheat
   b) shearing sheep
   c) pressing olives
   d) pressing grapes

4. What was Gideon's first test for the Lord?

5. What was Gideon's second test for the Lord?

6. Fill in the blanks: "The people are yet _____ _____; bring them down unto the _____."

7. The final number of men in Gideon's army was
    a) twenty-two thousand
    b) ten thousand
    c) five hundred
    d) three hundred

8. True or False: Gideon's army used drums and clubs to frighten and confuse the Midianite army.

9. What did Gideon's army shout?

10. True or False: The Lord confused the Midianites so that they attacked one another.

Quiz 49

Samson and Friends (and Enemies)

*The judge Samson would have fared well in a modern
"last man standing" contest. How much do you remember
about him and his exploits among the Philistines?*

1. Who was Samson's father?
   a) Samuel
   b) Elimelech
   c) Manoah
   d) Abraham

2. Choose A or B: Samson's riddle was based on A) a bear and honey B) a lion and honey.

3. Fill in the blank: Because his wife was given to someone else, Samson used three hundred _____ to burn up the Philistines crops.

4. How many times did Samson lie to Delilah about the source of his strength before he told her the truth?

5. What was the truth about the source of Samson's strength?

6. Choose A or B: Delilah betrayed Samson to the A) elders B) lords of the Philistines.

7. True or False: When the Philistines captured Samson, they treated him kindly.

8. The Philistines brought Samson to
    a) Gilead
    b) Gibeah
    c) Galilee
    d) Gaza

9. Fill in the blank: Samson was bound with fetters of _____.

10. True or False: Samson killed more Philistines at his death than he did during his life.

Quiz 50

The Story of Ruth

The book of Ruth contains one of the most inspirational love stories in the Bible. These questions should jog your memory about Ruth and her relatives.

1. Choose A or B: Naomi was Ruth's A) mother-in-law B) sister-in-law.

2. Ruth was from
    a) Moab
    b) Edom

c) Ammon

d) Canaan

3. Who said, "Thy people shall be my people"?

4. Ruth and Naomi dwelt in
    a) Bethlehem
    b) Jerusalem
    c) Jordan
    d) Galilee

5. Choose A or B: Naomi changed her name to Mara which meant A) "bitter" B) "blessed."

6. Whose field did Ruth glean in?
    a) David's field
    b) Chilion's field
    c) Mahlon's field
    d) Boaz's field

7. Choose A or B: Ruth showed Boaz her interest in him by A) tugging on his mantle B) sleeping at his feet.

8. True or False: Boaz was Naomi's closest living relative.

9. True or False: Naomi became nurse to Ruth's child.

10. Choose A or B: Ruth's child by Boaz was named A) Jesse B) Obed.

Introducing Samuel

*These questions deal with the early years
of the prophet Samuel in the book of
1 Samuel. How many can you answer?*

1. Choose A or B: When Eli saw Hannah praying, he thought she was A) devout B) drunk.

2. True or False: Hannah's husband, Elkanah, had another wife who was mean to Hannah.

3. Hannah called her son Samuel because
   a) it was a family name
   b) her husband told her to
   c) she had asked the Lord for a son
   d) Eli told her to

4. Hannah gave her son Samuel to the Lord
   a) after he reached his twelfth birthday
   b) as soon as he was circumcised
   c) as soon as he was weaned
   d) as soon as he was born

5. Choose A or B: Eli's sons A) followed in Eli's footsteps B) did not know the Lord.

6. Fill in the blank: Samuel grew and was in _____ with the Lord and also with man.

7. When the Lord called Samuel, what did Eli tell Samuel to reply?

8. Choose A or B: The Lord told Samuel that the sin of Eli's house A) shall B) shall not be purged with sacrifice.

9. Fill in the blank: Samuel _____ to show Eli the vision he had received about Eli's sons.

10. Who said, "It is the Lord: let him do what seemeth him good"?

Quiz 52

Philistine Trouble

A warlike people known as the Philistines troubled Israel during the ministry of the prophet Samuel. How much do you recall about these people?

1. Who took the ark of the covenant into battle with the Philistines?

2. Who said, "Woe unto us! Who shall deliver us out of the hands of these mighty Gods?"

3. True or False: When the ark was taken, Eli's sons were killed.

4. Choose A or B: When Eli heard that the ark was taken, he fell over backward and broke his A) back B) neck.

5. Who said, "The glory is departed from Israel"?

6. Choose A or B: The Philistines set the ark by their god, Dagon, and the next morning A) Dagon was gone B) Dagon was face down in front of the ark.

7. True or False: God struck the Philistines with leprosy because they took the ark.

8. The Philistines kept the ark how many months?
      a) three
      b) five
      c) seven
      d) nine

9. Fill in the blank: The Philistines sent the ark back to the Israelites on a _____.

10. The ark was brought to the house of
      a) the Lord
      b) Abinadab
      c) Samuel
      d) Eli

Quiz 53

Give Us a King!

*The Israelites demanded a king to lead
them because of the Philistine threat.
How did Samuel respond to their request?*

1. True or False: Samuel's sons were just as devout and obedient to the Lord as their father.

2. True or False: When Israel demanded a king, the Lord told Samuel, "They have not rejected thee, but they have rejected me."

3. Fill in the blank: When Saul met Samuel, Saul was looking for his father's _____.

4. Saul was of the tribe of
    a) Judah
    b) Reuben
    c) Levi
    d) Benjamin

5. Who said, "The Lord hath anointed thee to be captain over his inheritance"?

6. True or False: The spirit of God came upon Saul, and he prophesied.

7. Where did Samuel call the people together to present Saul as their king?
   - a) Bethlehem
   - b) Mizpeh
   - c) Jerusalem
   - d) Shiloh

8. True or False: Samuel wrote about the kingdom in a book.

9. Saul's first battle as king was against the
   - a) Philistines
   - b) Ammonites
   - c) Midianites
   - d) Edomites

10. True or False: Saul was formally proclaimed as king before the Lord in Bethel.

Quiz 54

A King in Trouble

Israel's first king, Saul, got off to a good start, but he soon got sidetracked and lost his influence. These questions show both the good and the bad about King Saul.

1. Who said, "Behold the king whom ye have chosen"?
   - a) Samuel
   - b) Eli

    c) Saul
    d) Jonathan

2. Choose A or B: Samuel rebuked Saul because Saul
   A) offered a burnt offering B) didn't kill all the enemies.

3. True or False: The Israelites had to go to the Philistines to get their iron tools sharpened.

4. When Saul decreed that no one in the army could eat until evening, who disobeyed him?

5. Who was the king of the Amalekites whom Saul left alive?
    a) Agag
    b) Elon
    c) Jabesh
    d) Sihon

6. Fill in the blank: "Behold, to _____ is better than sacrifice."

7. Who said, "Because thou hast rejected the word of the Lord, he hath also rejected thee from being king"?

8. True or False: When Samuel tried to leave Saul, Saul tore Samuel's garment.

9. Who killed the king of the Amalekites?

10. Fill in the blanks: "The Lord _____ that he had made _____ king over Israel."

Hello, David

The Lord chose David to replace Saul as king.
This quiz shows how his character, bravery, and God-
given abilities made him an ideal choice for the kingship.

1. Fill in the blanks: "Man looketh on the _____ appearance, but the Lord looketh on the _____."

2. David's father, Jesse, had how many sons?

3. When Samuel anointed David, what came upon David?

4. What was Saul troubled by after the Spirit of the Lord left him?
    a) stinging insects
    b) an evil spirit
    c) his disobedient sons
    d) a lack of sleep

5. True or False: David's first contact with Saul came about because David could play the harp.

6. Choose A or B: Goliath was A) an Amalekite B) a Philistine.

7. How many stones did David take from the brook?
    a) 1
    b) 3

c) 4
d) 5

8. Who said, "Am I a dog, that thou comest to me with staves?"

9. Whose sword did David use to cut off Goliath's head?

10. Choose A or B: David took Goliath's head to
   A) Bethlehem B) Jerusalem.

Quiz 56

Maniacal Monarch

King Saul's crazed jealousy of David is one of the most tragic events of the Bible. These questions show just how far off the mark his resentment took him.

1. Choose A or B: Jonathan loved David as his own A) soul B) friend.

2. True or False: Saul set David over the men of war.

3. Choose A or B: Saul was displeased with David because the A) men B) women cheered for David.

4. Fill in the blank: When the evil spirit came upon Saul, he threw a _____ at David.

5. Why was Saul afraid of David?
   a) because David was bigger than Saul
   b) because David hated Saul
   c) because David was plotting a rebellion against Saul
   d) because the Lord was with David

6. Choose A or B: Jonathan's sign to David about Saul's state of mind involved A) throwing a spear B) shooting arrows.

7. When Saul was chasing David, whose sword did David receive from Ahimelech?

8. When David had a chance to kill Saul, all David did was cut off part of Saul's
   a) robe
   b) hand
   c) little toe
   d) right ear

9. Who said, "The LORD forbid that I should stretch forth mine hand against the Lord's anointed"?

10. True or False: To escape Saul, David went and lived with the Philistines.

Quiz 57

Saul's Final Mistake

We're not surprised that King Saul met a tragic death.
These questions serve as a review of his final days.

1. Choose A or B: Saul went to see a medium, or fortune-teller, at Endor because A) he wanted some company B) he was afraid.

2. True or False: The spirit of Samuel appeared to Saul.

3. Who killed Saul's sons?
    a) the Amalekites
    b) the Philistines
    c) the Edomites
    d) the Jebusites

4. Choose A or B: Saul was wounded by A) a sword B) an arrow.

5. How did Saul die?

6. True or False: When Saul's armourbearer saw that Saul was dead, the armourbearer killed himself.

7. True or False: When the enemies found Saul's body, they buried it on the battlefield.

8. How many of Saul's sons were killed with him?
    a) one   c) three
    b) five   d) seven

9. Fill in the blank: The _____ men from Jabesh-Gilead arose and went at night to retrieve the bodies of Saul and his sons.

10. The men burned the bones of Saul and his sons and fasted how many days?
    a) one
    b) three
    c) five
    d) seven

Quiz 58

King David

This quiz from 2 Samuel shows David in the early days of his kingship. What do they tell us about his personality and leadership qualities?

1. True or False: David praised and rewarded the young man who took credit for killing Saul.

2. David was anointed King of Judah in what city?
    a) Bethlehem
    b) Hebron
    c) Jerusalem
    d) Shiloh

3. Who made Saul's son, Ishbosheth, king over Israel?
   - a) Abner
   - b) the Lord
   - c) David
   - d) a priest

4. After Ishbosheth was dead, who anointed David king over Israel?

5. Choose A or B: When David brought the ark of the covenant on a cart to Jerusalem, A) Uzzah B) Ahio touched the ark and died.

6. Fill in the blank: David's wife, Michal, was the daughter of _____.

7. The prophet who came to David soon after he became king was
   - a) Elijah
   - b) Elisha
   - c) Nathan
   - d) Obadiah

8. Choose A or B: Mephibosheth was the son of A) Saul B) Jonathan.

9. True or False: David was kind to Mephibosheth.

10. Fill in the blanks: "Mephibosheth. . .did _____ continually at the _____ _____."

Royal Scandal

*Even King David wasn't perfect.
How much do you recall about his great sin
and his attempts at a "royal cover-up"?*

1. True or False: When David first saw Bathsheba she was taking a bath.

2. Bathsheba's husband, Uriah, was a
    a) Hittite
    b) Ammonite
    c) Philistine
    d) Syrian

3. True or False: David confessed to Uriah that he, the king, had committed adultery with Uriah's wife and gotten her pregnant.

4. Choose A or B: David sent a letter to A) Joab B) Abner with Uriah.

5. The letter said Uriah was to be
    a) honored
    b) rewarded
    c) put at the front of the battle
    d) sent home again

6. What happened to Uriah?

7. Who told David the story of the man with one ewe lamb?

8. True or False: The Lord told David that because of David's sin, the baby born to David and Bathsheba would die.

9. Who said, "I shall go to him, but he shall not return to me"?

10. What was the name of David and Bathsheba's second son?
   a) Absalom
   b) Adonijah
   c) Nathan
   d) Solomon

Quiz 60

A Family Unravels

Family problems haunted David during the latter years of his reign. These questions have a message about the lingering effects of sin.

1. Choose A or B: Tamar was Absalom's A) sister B) cousin.

2. True or False: Amnon, David's son, fell in love with Shamgar.

3. How did Amnon trick Tamar into coming to his chambers?

4. When Absalom found out that Amnon had dishonored Tamar, how long did Absalom wait before he killed Amnon?
   a) no time
   b) six months
   c) two years
   d) five years

5. After he killed Amnon, to where did Absalom flee?
   a) Bethlehem
   b) Canaan
   c) Jordan
   d) Geshur

6. Who did David send to bring Absalom out of exile?

7. Fill in the blanks: "In all Israel there was none to be so much _____ as Absalom for his _____."

8. How long did Absalom dwell in Jerusalem before he was allowed to see his father?

9. True or False: Absalom patiently waited for his father, David, to die so he could succeed him as king.

10. True or False: Absalom got his head caught in a tree, and that's how Joab found him and killed him.

Quiz 61

From David to Solomon

The transition from David's reign to the kingship of his son, Solomon, did not go flawlessly. See how many of these transition complications you can sort out.

1. Fill in the blank: Adonijah, who tried to take over as king before David died, was the brother of _____.

2. True or False: The captain of David's army, Joab, helped Adonijah.

3. Who said to David, "Thou swarest by the Lord thy God unto thine handmaid, saying, Assuredly Solomon thy son shall reign after me"?

4. Fill in the blanks: David had _____ the priest and _____ the prophet declare Solomon king.

5. True or False: Because Adonijah was afraid of Solomon, he went and took hold of the ark of the covenant.

6. Who said, "If he will shew himself a worthy man, there shall not an hair of him fall to the earth"?

7. How many years did David rule over Israel from Hebron?
    a) twenty-seven
    b) seven

c) forty-seven

d) fifty-seven

8. To whom did Adonijah go with his request to marry David's concubine?

9. True or False: Solomon had Adonijah put to death because of his request to marry David's concubine.

10. Solomon sent Benaiah to kill whom?
    a) Abner
    b) Joab
    c) Anathoth
    d) Zeruiah

Quiz 62

Wisdom, Please

King Solomon's reign started well with his request for wisdom from the Lord. How did God answer his request?

1. Choose A or B: Solomon married the daughter of A) Pharaoh B) King Hiram.

2. Which of the following was *not* something Solomon was building?
    a) his house
    b) the house of the Lord

c) an aqueduct

d) a wall around Jerusalem

3. Fill in the blank: "Solomon _____ the LORD, walking in the statutes of David his father."

4. Choose A or B: The Lord appeared to Solomon in a
A) vision B) dream.

5. In what city did the Lord appear to Solomon in a dream?
a) Jerusalem
b) Gibeon
c) Samaria
d) Hebron

6. True or False: Solomon told the Lord, "I am but a little child."

7. Solomon asked the Lord, "Give therefore thy servant an _____ heart."
a) understanding
b) humble
c) egotistical
d) honorable

8. Choose A or B: The Lord was A) pleased B) displeased with Solomon's request.

9. Two women with a dispute were brought to Solomon. What were they quarreling about?

10. How did Solomon solve the problem?

Temple Builder

*King Solomon inherited the task of building the temple
from his father, David. How many questions
about its construction can you answer?*

1. True or False: David was given permission by the Lord to build the temple.

2. Fill in the blank: Solomon got the cedars of Lebanon to use in building the temple from King _____ of Tyre.

3. How were the trees sent from Lebanon to Solomon?

4. Fill in the blank: The Lord gave Solomon _____ as he had promised him.

5. Choose A or B: The temple windows were A) narrow B) wide.

6. Fill in the blanks: God promised Solomon, "I will _____ among the children of Israel, and will not _____ my people Israel."

7. Fill in the blank: The inside of the house of the Lord was overlaid with _____.

8. Choose A or B: The figures inside the oracle where the ark of the covenant was placed were A) seraphim B) cherubim.

9. Which of the following was not carved on the doors of the temple?
    a) lions
    b) cherubim
    c) flowers
    d) palm trees

10. Who brought the ark of the covenant into the temple after it was completed?
    a) Solomon's army
    b) Solomon himself
    c) the priests
    d) the scribes

Quiz 64

Solomon's Glory

The Lord blessed Solomon with great wealth and power. Just how glorious was the kingdom over which he ruled?

1. Choose A or B: The Lord told Solomon that if Solomon would A) pray B) walk uprightly, the Lord would establish his kingdom forever.

2. What would happen if Solomon or his children did not keep the Lord's commandments?

3. Which of the following did Solomon make bondservants?
    a) Hittites
    b) Hivites
    c) Jebusites
    d) all of the above

4. How many times a year did Solomon offer burnt offerings and peace offerings to the Lord?

5. The queen who came to see Solomon was the queen of
    a) Ethiopia
    b) Samaria
    c) Egypt
    d) Sheba

6. Fill in the blank: The queen saw all of Solomon's _____.

7. Fill in the blank: The queen brought Solomon an abundance of _____, _____ _____, and _____.

8. True or False: The weight of the gold that came to Solomon every year was six hundred threescore and six talents.

9. Fill in the blank: Solomon's throne was made of _____ overlaid with gold.

10. What carvings stood on each side of Solomon's throne?
    a) six sheep
    b) twelve lions
    c) three seraphim
    d) two cherubim

Wise and Foolish

*The king known for his wisdom also made some
foolish mistakes. This quiz points out what these
mistakes were and shows their consequences.*

1. Fill in the blank: "King Solomon _____ many strange women."

2. True or False: These women came from nations the Lord
   had told Israel not to mingle with.

3. Fill in the blank: The women turned Solomon's heart unto
   their _____.

4. True or False: Solomon had three hundred wives and seven
   concubines.

5. Choose A or B: Solomon did A) right B) evil in the sight of
   the Lord.

6. True or False: Solomon built high places for the pagan gods
   Chemosh and Molech.

7. Fill in the blanks: The Lord told Solomon, "Forsasmuch
   as. . .thou hast not kept my _____ and my _____. . .
   I will surely _____ the _____ from thee."

8. Solomon's enemy, Hadad, was from
   a) Edom
   b) Egypt

c) Moab

d) Ammon

9. The prophet Ahijah told Jeroboam that the Lord would give him how many tribes to rule over?
   a) two
   b) ten
   c) seven
   d) twelve

10. Fill in the blank: When Solomon heard what Ahijah had told Jeroboam, Solomon tried to _____ Jeroboam.

Quiz 66

A Kingdom Divided

The names Rehoboam and Jeroboam may sound alike.
But they were two different people who were associated
with the split of Solomon's united kingdom.
Try to sort them out in this quiz.

1. To which city did Rehoboam go to be made king?
   a) Gibeon
   b) Jerusalem
   c) Shechem
   d) Bethlehem

2. Choose A or B: Jeroboam heard of this while he was in
   A) Tyre B) Egypt.

3. True or False: Rehoboam accepted the counsel of the old
   men.

4. Fill in the blank: Rehoboam told the people, "My father
   also chastised you with whips, but I will chastise you with
   _____."

5. Choose A or B: Rehoboam reigned over the cities of
   A) Judah B) Israel.

6. When Rehoboam sent Adoram among the northern tribes
   to collect tribute, what happened to Adoram?

7. True or False: After what happened in Question 6,
   Rehoboam had to flee to Jerusalem.

8. Who made two calves of gold for the people to worship?

9. The two golden calves were put in
     a) Sodom and Gomorrah
     b) Jerusalem and Bethlehem
     c) Bethel and Dan
     d) Bethsaida and Capernaum

10. How many years did Rehoboam rule in Judah?
      a) ten
      b) thirteen
      c) seventeen
      d) twenty-one

Quiz 67

The Prophet Elijah

This prophet took a courageous stand for the Lord in spite of opposition from the king and queen. See how much you remember about his life and ministry.

1. Fill in the blank: When Elijah hid by the brook of Cherith, the Lord sent him food by _____.

2. True or False: Because the widow of Zarephath gave Elijah the last of her food, the Lord made her barrel of meal and cruse of oil unending until the drought was over.

3. True or False: When the widow's son died, Elijah raised him back to life.

4. Elijah met the prophets of Baal on Mount
    a) Moriah
    b) Carmel
    c) Nebo
    d) Hor

5. Fill in the blank: Elijah built his altar on Mount Carmel of _____ stones.

6. True or False: Elijah poured one barrel of water over his altar and the sacrifice.

7. Fill in the blank: The fire of the Lord consumed the burnt sacrifices, the wood, the stones, the dust, and the _____.

8. When Elijah fled from Jezebel, what did God send to feed him?

9. The Lord told Elijah, "I have left me _____ _____ in Israel, all the knees which have not bowed unto Baal."
   a) five hundred
   b) three thousand
   c) one thousand
   d) seven thousand

10. When Elijah found Elisha, the prophet Elisha was
    a) plowing
    b) eating
    c) praying
    d) singing

Quiz 68

Ahab and Jezebel

This royal couple was evil personified. But these questions show how they eventually got what they deserved.

1. True or False: Naboth refused to sell his vineyard to Ahab because it was Naboth's inheritance.

2. Fill in the blank: "[Ahab] laid him down upon his bed, and turned away his face, and would eat no _____."

3. Who said, "I will give thee the vineyard of Naboth"?

4. True or False: Jezebel's strategy for getting Naboth's vineyard was to offer him three times what it was worth.

5. Naboth was executed by being
   a) beheaded
   b) stoned
   c) stabbed
   d) beaten

6. What prophet did God send to rebuke Ahab?

7. Why did Ahab hate the prophet Micaiah?

8. True or False: Ahab disguised himself before he went into battle so the enemy would not recognize him as the king of Israel.

9. Ahab was buried in
   a) Jerusalem
   b) Bethlehem
   c) Samaria
   d) Judea

10. Fill in the blank: When Ahab's chariot was washed, the dogs licked up his _____, according to the word of the Lord.

Quiz 69

The Prophet Elisha

Elisha's ministry seemed to consist of one miracle after another. See how many of them you remember by answering these questions.

1. Fill in the blank: Elisha saw Elijah taken up by a _____ into heaven.

2. True or False: Elisha used the mantle of Elijah to divide the waters of the Jordan River.

3. Choose A or B: When children called Elisha a bald-head, God sent two A) bears B) lions to punish them.

4. True or False: When a widow came to Elisha for help, he multiplied her flour to fill all the pots she borrowed from her neighbors.

5. Fill in the blank: Elisha raised the son of a _____ woman from the dead.

6. Naaman was the captain of the hosts of the king of
    a) Egypt
    b) Syria
    c) Damascus
    d) Tyre

7. True or False: When Elisha told Naaman to dip seven times in the Jordan River to cure his leprosy, Naaman grew angry.

8. When Elisha's servant, Gehazi, lied to Naaman and took the treasures that Elisha had refused, what was Gehazi's punishment?

9. What did Elisha cause to float on the water?
   a) an empty pot
   b) an ax head
   c) a stone
   d) a scroll

10. Fill in the blank: When the Syrians surrounded the city Elisha was in, the Lord surrounded the city with _____ of fire.

Quiz 70

Royally Bad

*Israel (the Northern Kingdom) had plenty of bad kings,
but these guys were some of the worst.
Sort them out with this quiz.*

1. Fill in the blank: "Ahaziah. . .walked in the way of the house of Ahab, and did _____ in the sight of the Lord."

2. What prophet told his follower to anoint Jehu king over Israel?

3. Choose A or B: The Lord told Jehu to A) smite the house of Ahab B) go to war against Egypt.

4. True or False: King Joram ordered that Jezebel be killed.

5. Fill in the blanks: Jereboam II "_____ _____ from all the sins of Jereboam the son of Nebat, who made Israel to sin."

6. How long did Shallum reign?
    a) a year
    b) a month
    c) a week
    d) a day

7. Choose A or B: Pekahiah was king of Israel for two years before being killed by A) his son B) a captain of his army.

8. True or False: In the days of Pekah, the king of Assyria came and carried off all the land of Naphtali into captivity.

9. Who made Hoshea, king of Israel, his servant?
    a) Nebuchadnezzar, king of Babylon
    b) Shadrach, king of Persia
    c) Shalmaneser, king of Assyria
    d) Thutmose, pharaoh of Egypt

10. True or False: Solomon was the last king of Israel before Israel was carried off into captivity.

Three Good Kings

Judah (the Southern Kingdom) was blessed with many
good kings, but these three guys were the best
of the best. Sort them out with this quiz.

1. Who hid Joash from his grandmother, Athaliah, when Athaliah killed all of her grandchildren so she could become queen?

2. How old was Joash (Jehoash) when he became king?

3. True or False: Joash (Jehoash) took up a collection from the people to repair his royal palace.

4. Fill in the blank: Hezekiah "did that which was _____ in the sight of the Lord."

5. True or False: Hezekiah broke up the brasen serpent that Moses had made.

6. Hezekiah
   a) departed not from following the Lord
   b) trusted in the Lord
   c) clave unto the Lord
   d) all of the above

7. True or False: The Lord delivered Hezekiah from Sennacherib, the king of Assyria, by sending an angel of the Lord to strike Sennacherib's army with a mysterious plague.

8. How old was Josiah when he began to reign?
- a) seventeen years old
- b) eight years old
- c) twenty years old
- d) twelve years old

9. Choose A or B: While the house of the Lord was being repaired in King Josiah's time, a priest found A) the book of the law B) the ark of the covenant.

10. King Josiah stood in the house of the Lord and made a covenant to
- a) walk after the Lord
- b) keep all the Lord's commandments
- c) perform the words of the covenant
- d) all of the above

Quiz 72

The End of the Line

*Both Judah (the Southern Kingdom) and Israel
(the Northern Kingdom) eventually fell to
foreign invaders. Review these tragic chapters
in their histories with these questions.*

1. The king of what country carried Israel off into captivity?
- a) Egypt
- b) Tyre
- c) Assyria
- d) Samaria

2. Fill in the blank: The people of Israel "walked in the statutes of the _____."

3. Choose A or B: The people of Israel "did A) secretly B) openly those things that were not right against the Lord."

4. Which of the following were the people of Israel *not* worshipping?
    a) two calves   c) Baal
    b) all the host of heaven   d) the Lord their God

5. True or False: The king who took the Israelites captive allowed a priest to teach them to fear the Lord.

6. The King of Judah who rebelled against the king of Babylon was
    a) Zedekiah   c) Jehoash
    b) Jedediah   d) Ahaziah

7. Fill in the blank: The king of Babylon who took Judah captive was _____.

8. What punishment did the king of Babylon inflict upon the king of Judah?
    a) killed his sons before his eyes   c) bound him with fetters of brass
    b) put his eyes out   d) all of the above

9. True or False: The king of Babylon burned down the house of the Lord in Jerusalem.

10. True or False: None of the people of Judah were left in the land.

Quiz 73

Temple Rebuilders

*The citizens of Judah (the Southern Kingdom)
were eventually allowed to return to their home-
land to rebuild the temple. See how much you
remember about this important event.*

1. The king of Persia who made the proclamation to allow
   God's people to go back to Jerusalem was

       a) Belteshazzar   c) Cyrus

       b) Hazael   d) Darius

2. True or False: The three tribes of Israel that went back to
   Jerusalem were Judah, Benjamin, and Levi.

3. Fill in the blank: The king of Persia "brought forth the
   _____ of the house of the Lord, which Nebuchadnezzar
   had brought forth out of Jerusalem."

4. Choose A or B: The first thing the Israelites built after re-
   turning to Jerusalem was A) an altar B) the wall of the city.

5. Fill in the blanks: "The people of the land _____ the hands
   of the people of Judah, and _____ them in building."

6. True or False: Some people wrote a letter to King
   Artaxerxes of Persia, accusing the inhabitants of Jerusalem
   of building a rebellious and bad city.

7. Fill in the blank: The Jews were made to _____ building "by force and power."

8. The two prophets prophesying in Jerusalem at this time were
    a) Isaiah and Jeremiah
    b) Habakkuk and Zephaniah
    c) Hosea and Joel
    d) Haggai and Zechariah

9. Who began to build the house of God again?
    a) Zerubbabel   c) Jeshua
    b) Iddo   d) a and c

10. True or False: King Darius issued a decree forbidding the rebuilding of the house of God.

Quiz 74

Ezra the Priest

Ezra played a key role in rebuilding the nation of Judah after the exile. These questions focus on his life and ministry.

1. Fill in the blank: Ezra was a "ready _____ in the law of Moses."

2. Ezra went to Jerusalem during the reign of
    a) Artaxerxes   c) Daniel
    b) Darius   d) Nebuchadnezzar

3. Fill in the blank: "Ezra had prepared his heart to seek the
    ____ of the Lord, and to do it."

4. True or False: The king gave Ezra a decree that said that
    everyone who wanted to go of their own free will to
    Jerusalem could go with Ezra.

5. Fill in the blank: The king of Persia and his counselors
    _____ _____ silver and gold "unto the God of Israel."

6. Choose A or B: The first offering the returnees made
    when they got to Jerusalem was a A) burnt offering
    B) peace offering.

7. Fill in the blank: Ezra _____ and confessed and cast himself
    down before the house of God.

8. What did the people do in response to Ezra's actions in
    question 7?
        a) they laughed   c) they wept
        b) they scowled   d) they rejoiced

9. True or False: Ezra ate no bread nor drank any water
    because he mourned over the sin of the people.

10. Ezra told the people, "Make confession unto the Lord God
    of your fathers, and do his _____."

Introducing Nehemiah

*Nehemiah led a reconstruction project in the city
of Jerusalem after the exile. Review the big job
he took on by answering these questions.*

1. Nehemiah wept when he heard that
   a) the remnant of Israelites in Jerusalem were afflicted
   b) the wall of Jerusalem was broken down
   c) the gates of Jerusalem were burned
   d) all of the above

2. Choose A or B: Nehemiah was the king's A) baker
   B) cupbearer.

3. True or False: Darius was king of Persia when Nehemiah
   was in captivity.

4. True or False: The king said Nehemiah could go to
   Jerusalem but that he had to return.

5. Fill in the blanks: A letter was given to Nehemiah to
   present to Asaph, the keeper of the king's _____ so Asaph
   would give Nehemiah _____.

6. Choose A or B: The king sent A) captains and horsemen
   B) builders and workmen with Nehemiah.

7. True or False: Nehemiah went out during the daytime to survey the ruins of Jerusalem's wall.

8. Who said, "Let us rise up and build"?

9. Fill in the blank: Sanballat, Tobiah, and Geshem laughed the Jewish builders to scorn and_____ them.

10. The people whom Nehemiah told that they had no portion, right, or memorial in Jerusalem were Sanballat, Tobiah, and
    a) Zerubbabel   c) Ezra
    b) Geshem   d) Urijah

Quiz 76

Putting Up Walls

Nehemiah led the people of Judah to rebuild the defensive wall around Jerusalem. This quiz shows how the task was accomplished.

1. Choose A or B: Eliashib the high priest and his priests built the A) sheep gate B) east gate.

2. Choose A or B: The sons of Hassenaah built the A) north gate B) fish gate.

3. True or False: The nobles of the Tekoites did not do the Lord's work.

4. Choose A or B: Hanun and the inhabitants of Zanoah repaired the A) south gate B) valley gate.

5. Fill in the blanks: Nehemiah set people in the _____ and on the _____ places behind the wall with swords, spears, and bows.

6. Who said, "Ye exact usury, every one of his brother"?

7. True or False: The nobles and rulers agreed to restore to the people their lands.

8. True or False: When Sanballat and Geshem asked Nehemiah to leave his work and come meet with them, Nehemiah agreed.

9. The wall was finished in
   a) fifty-two days
   b) seventy-five days
   c) ninety days
   d) a year.

10. Who did Nehemiah put in charge of opening and shutting the gates of Jerusalem and guarding the city?
   a) Hanani and Hananiah
   b) Shadrach and Meshach
   c) Daniel and Joel
   d) Matthew and Mark

Quiz 77

Call for a Queen

This quiz might be titled, "How a Jewish Girl Became Queen of Persia." These questions show how it happened.

1. Who was the queen in Persia before Esther was named to that position?

2. The king was angry with the Queen Vashti
    a) because she was still in bed
    b) because she had insulted him the day before
    c) because she had fired one of his servants
    d) because she refused to appear before his guests

3. Who said, "What shall we do unto the queen. . .according to law?"

4. True or False: The queen had to be punished because the king was afraid her action would cause wives to despise their husbands.

5. Who suggested that the king replace the queen?
    a) the elders
    b) his servants
    c) his counselors
    d) the satraps

6. True or False: Esther's Hebrew name was Marsena.

7. Mordecai was Esther's
   a) uncle
   b) cousin
   c) father
   d) brother

8. Fill in the blank: Hegai was the king's keeper of the _____.

9. True or False: Esther didn't tell anyone at the king's palace that she was Jewish.

10. Fill in the blank: "And the king _____ Esther above all the women."

Quiz 78

Attempted Holocaust

God used Esther and Mordecai to save His people from a mass murder plot. Answer these questions to see how God worked His plan.

1. Fill in the blank: Haman was "_____ all the princes that were with him."

2. Haman was angry because Mordecai
   a) mocked him
   b) told lies about him

     c) wouldn't bow down to him

     d) had stolen a horse from him

3. True or False: Since Mordecai was a Jew, Haman decided to destroy only the members of Mordecai's family.

4. True or False: Esther's life was in danger if she appeared before the king without being summoned.

5. Fill in the blank: When Esther appeared before the king, he held out his golden _____ to her.

6. To what did Esther invite the king and Haman?

7. The king sought to reward Mordecai because Mordecai
     a) was an honorable man
     b) was Esther's relative
     c) had saved the king's life
     d) hated Haman

8. True or False: Haman was forced to lead Mordecai through the streets on horseback and proclaim that the king was honoring Mordecai.

9. Who told the king that Haman was trying to destroy all the Jews?
     a) Mordecai
     b) Esther
     c) the king's servants
     d) Haman's wife

10. Choose A or B: Haman was A) hanged B) beheaded.

Quiz 79

Job Under Attack

Who was Job, and how was his faith tested?
This quiz is designed to help you answer these questions.

1. Who went before God and charged that Job served the Lord for selfish reasons?
   a) Satan
   b) Eliphaz
   c) Job's wife
   d) Bildad

2. True or False: While one servant was telling Job that the Chaldeans had taken his camels, another servant came up and told Job that his children had been killed.

3. Fill in the blank: "The Lord gave, and the Lord hath taken away; _____ be the name of the Lord."

4. Who smote Job with boils, or sores?

5. Fill in the blanks: Job took a _____ to scrape himself with and sat down among the _____.

6. Who told Job to "curse God, and die"?
   a) Zophar
   b) Job's daughter
   c) Satan
   d) Job's wife

7. Fill in the blank: "In all this did not Job _____ with his lips."

8. What were the names of Job's friends who came to comfort him?

9. When Job's friends came they
   a) wept
   b) rent their mantles
   c) sprinkled dust upon their heads
   d) all of the above

10. How many days and nights did Job's friends sit with him without saying a word?
   a) three
   b) seven
   c) one
   d) five

Quiz 80

Friends, So-Called

Contrary to popular thinking, Job was not a silent, patient sufferer. These questions show how he responded to his pain and to those who tried to comfort him.

1. Who broke the silence after Job's friends came to comfort him?

2. True or False: Bildad spoke second.

3. Who said, "How long shall the words of thy mouth be like a strong wind?"

4. Zophar said,
    a) "Should not the multitude of words be answered?"
    b) "Oh that God would speak."
    c) "Canst thou by searching find out God?"
    d) all of the above

5. Who said, "Though he slay me, yet will I trust in him"?

6. True or False: Bildad said, "How long will it be ere ye make an end of words?"

7. The three men "ceased to answer Job, because he was _____ in his own eyes."
    a) superior
    b) innocent
    c) righteous
    d) honored

8. Fill in the blank: Elihu's wrath was kindled against Job because Job _____ himself rather than God.

9. Choose A or B: Elihu waited to speak because A) the others were older than him B) he was afraid to speak up.

10. Who was the last person to speak before God spoke?
    a) Job   c) Bildad
    b) Zophar   d) Elihu

Quiz 81

God Breaks His Silence

*After listening to Job for a long time, God finally
answered his complaints. Find out what He
had to say by answering these questions.*

1. The Lord answered Job out of
    a) a whirlwind
    b) heaven
    c) an earthquake
    d) a thunderstorm

2. Fill in the blank: "Where wast thou when I laid the _____
of the earth?"

3. God asked where Job was when all the morning stars
    a) sang
    b) shone brightly
    c) were created
    d) fell from the sky

4. Fill in the blank: "All the sons of God shouted for _____."

5. Fill in the blank: "Doth the hawk fly by thy _____?"

6. Who said, "I will lay mine hand upon my mouth"?

7. God told Job, "Wilt thou condemn me, that thou mayest be _____?"
   a) justified
   b) righteous
   c) saved
   d) condemned

8. Fill in the blank: "Canst thou draw out leviathan with an _____?"

9. Fill in the blank: "Whatsoever is under the whole _____ is mine."

10. Fill in the blank: "Upon earth there is not his _____, who is made without fear."

Quiz 82

The Wrap on Job

*What happened to Job after all his speeches
were over and God answered his complaints?
This quiz brings Job's story to a happy conclusion.*

1. Fill in the blank: "No _____ can be withholden from thee."

2. Whom was the Lord's wrath kindled against?
   a) Eliphaz
   b) Bildad
   c) Zophar
   d) all of the above

3. True or False: Job spoke of the Lord the thing that is right.

4. What did the Lord tell Job to do for his friends?

5. Fill in the blank: "The LORD gave Job _____ as much as he had before."

6. Who came to comfort Job?
   a) all his brethren
   b) all his sisters
   c) all who knew him
   d) all of the above

7. True or False: Everyone gave Job a bracelet of gold.

8. Fill in the blanks: "The LORD blessed the _____ end of Job more than his _____."

9. True or False: Job had seven sons and three daughters.

10. Job saw his sons' sons unto how many generations?
    a) two
    b) three
    c) four
    d) five

Quiz 83

Everyone's Favorite Psalm

So you think you know the Twenty-third Psalm?
Find out if you do by answering these questions.

1. Fill in the blank: "The Lord is my shepherd; I shall not
   _____."

2. True or False: God leads us beside still waters before He
   makes us lie down in green pastures.

3. What does God do to our souls?
   a) creates them
   b) berates them
   c) restores them
   d) praises them

4. Choose A or B: "He leadeth me in the A) paths B) ways of
   righteousness for his name's sake."

5. Fill in the blanks: "Yea, though I walk through the _____
   of the _____ of death, I will fear no _____."

6. True or False: "Thy rod and thy staff they comfort me."

7. What is prepared "before me in the presence of mine
   enemies"?
   a) a lamp   c) a scroll
   b) a desk   d) a table

8. Fill in the blank: "Thou _____ my head with oil."

9. What will "follow me all the days of my life"?
   a) goodness and mercy
   b) fear and dread
   c) happiness and joy
   d) duty and responsibility

10. Fill in the blank: "I will _____ in the house of the Lord for ever."

Quiz 84

Psalms Fill-in-the-Blanks, Part 1

The Psalms contain some of the most-quoted verses in the Bible. Test your "quotation I.Q." of the Psalms with these questions.

1. "_____ is the man that walketh not in the council of the ungodly."

2. "O Lord, our Lord, how _____ is thy name in all the earth!"

3. "The _____ hath said in his heart, There is no God."
   a) knave
   b) fool
   c) sinner
   d) demented

4. "The testimony of the Lord is sure, making _____ the simple."

5. "The Lord is my _____ and my _____."

6. "I will _____ thee and teach thee in the way which thou shalt go."

7. "Delight thyself also in the LORD: and he shall give thee the _____ of thine _____."
   a) joy, salvation
   b) fullness, wishes
   c) desires, heart
   d) answer, prayer

8. "Be still, and _____ that I am God."

9. "Create in me a _____ heart, O God; and renew a right _____ within me."

10. "I will _____ the works of the LORD."

Quiz 85

Psalms Fill-in-the-Blanks, Part 2

*See if you can do better than you did on Quiz 84
with these additional questions on the Psalms.
On your mark, get set, go. . . .*

1. "Lord, thou hast been our _____ _____ in all generations."
   a) wonderful Saviour
   b) decorated crown
   c) mighty rock
   d) dwelling place

2. "I will say of the Lord, He is my _____ and my fortress."

3. "Serve the Lord with _____: come before his presence with _____."

4. "I will _____ of mercy and judgment: unto thee, O Lord, will I _____."

5. "_____ the Lord, O my soul: and all that is within me, _____ his holy name."

6. "The Lord shall _____ thee from all evil: he shall _____ thy soul."

7. "Lo, children are an _____ of the Lord."

8. "O lord, thou hast searched me, and _____ me."
   a) known
   b) honored
   c) condemned
   d) questioned

9. "The Lord is _____ to all."

10. "Let every thing that hath breath _____ the LORD."

Quiz 86

Psalm 119

This psalm is the longest chapter in the Bible—176 verses!
Aren't you glad this quiz doesn't require you
to quote the whole thing from memory?

1. True or False: Every verse of Psalm 119 makes some reference to the law of the Lord.

2. Fill in the blank: "_____ are the undefiled in the way."

3. Why did the psalmist hide God's word in his heart?

4. "For ever, O LORD, thy ____ is settled in heaven."
    a) word
    b) testimony
    c) statute
    d) covenant

5. Fill in the blank: "O how ____ I thy law."

6. Fill in the blanks: "Thy word is a ____ unto my feet, and a ____ unto my path."

7. Choose A or B: "Thy testimonies have I taken as
   A) an heritage B) a covenant for ever."

8. Fill in the blank: "Thou art my ____ place and my shield."

9. "Righteous art thou, O LORD, and ____ are thy judgments."
    a) true
    b) upright
    c) wonderful
    d) everlasting

10. Choose A or B: "Thy righteousness is A) an everlasting
    B) a merciful righteousness."

More from the Psalms

In case you've lost count, this is quiz number five on the Psalms. Hang in there! You will be rewarded with a greater appreciation for these expressions of praise to the Lord.

1. Psalm 2 wonders why the _____ rage.
   a) peoples
   b) nations
   c) heathen
   d) adversaries

2. Fill in the blank: "_____ belongeth unto the Lord."

3. Choose A or B: "Offer the A) sacrifices
   B) faith of righteousness, and put your trust in the LORD."

4. Who shall abide in the Lord's tabernacle?
   a) He that walketh uprightly.
   b) He that worketh righteousness.
   c) He that speaketh the truth in his heart.
   d) all of the above

5. Fill in the blank: "The heavens declare the _____ of God."

6. Choose A or B: "Let me not be ashamed, let not mine
   A) enemies B) faults triumph over me."

7. Fill in the blank: "I have been young, and now am old; yet I have not seen the _____ forsaken."

8. Choose A or B: "I waited A) quietly B) patiently for the Lord."

9. Fill in the blank: "As the hart panteth after the water brooks, so panteth my _____ after thee, O God."

10. "Why art thou cast down, O my _____? and why art thou _____ within me?"
     a) thoughts, confused
     b) head, aching
     c) joy, hopeless
     d) soul, disquieted

Quiz 88

And Yet More from the Psalms

Just when you thought you were finished with the Psalms, here's more! But after all, it is the longest book in the Bible.

1. Choose A or B: "Wash me, and I shall be whiter than A) wool B) snow."

2. "In God is. . ."
    a) "my salvation."
    b) "my glory."
    c) "the rock of my strength."
    d) all of the above

3. Fill in the blank: "O God, thou art my God; _____ will I seek thee."

4. Choose A or B: "Sing forth the A) honour B) glory of his name."

5. Choose A or B: "Give the A) king B) people thy judgments, O God."

6. Fill in the blank: "Truly God is good to. . .such as are of a clean _____."

7. True or False: God will teach us to number our days, so we may apply our hearts to wisdom.

8. Fill in the blank: "_____ thou the work of our hands upon us."

9. Choose A or B: "It is a A) good B) righteous thing to give thanks unto the Lord."

10. Which one of the following musical instruments does Psalm 150 not specifically refer to?
    a) violin   c) psaltery
    b) trumpet   d) timbrel

Quiz 89

Proverbially Speaking, Part 1

All of us can use more wisdom.
So settle in for a long review of Proverbs,
known as one of the wisdom books of the Bible.

1. True or False: The book of Proverbs begins with the proverbs of Solomon.

2. Choose A or B: "The A) fear B) glory of the Lord is the beginning of knowledge."

3. Fill in the blank: "My son, if _____ entice thee, consent thou not."

4. According to Proverbs 2:11, what will preserve people?
    a) wisdom
    b) understanding
    c) discretion
    d) knowledge

5. Fill in the blanks: "_____ in the Lord with all thine heart, and lean not unto thine own _____."

6. Choose A or B: "Honor the Lord with thy A) heart B) substance."

7. "Happy is the man that findeth _____."
    a) home   c) wisdom
    b) money   d) children

8. True or False: "The curse of the Lord is in the house of the wicked."

9. Fill in the blank: "Hear, ye children, the _____ of a father."

10. Fill in the blank: "Keep thy heart with all _____; for out of it are the issues of _____."
    a) diligence, life   c) care, peace
    b) wisdom, joy   d) patience, reward

Quiz 90

Proverbially Speaking, Part 2

*More wisdom is coming your way
in this quiz. Don't you agree that wisdom
is something we can use more of?*

1. Choose A or B: "My son, attend unto my wisdom, and bow thine A) ear B) heart to my understanding."

2. True or False: "The lips of a strange woman drop as an honeycomb."

3. True or False: The feet of a strange woman "go down to death."

4. Fill in the blank: "Go to the ____, thou sluggard; consider her ways, and be wise."

5. There are seven things that are an abomination to the Lord. Which of the following is *not* one of them?
   a) a lying tongue
   b) hands that shed innocent blood
   c) a proud look
   d) a haughty heart

6. Fill in the blank: "My son, keep thy father's commandment, and forsake not the law of thy _____."

7. Fill in the blank: "Can a man take fire in his bosom, and his clothes not be _____?"

8. Where does wisdom stand to cry out?
   a) the top of the high places
   b) the places of the paths
   c) the entry of the city
   d) all of the above

9. Choose A or B: Receive God's instruction, and not A) silver B) gold.

10. True or False: Wisdom did not develop until the time of Abraham.

Quiz 91

Proverbially Speaking, Part 3

Are you beginning to think you're suffering from wisdom overload? Not yet. Proverbs still has some wisdom to teach you.

1. A foolish woman
    a) is clamorous
    b) is simple
    c) knoweth nothing
    d) all of the above

2. Fill in the blank: "A _____ son maketh a glad father."

3. Choose A or B: "The A) memory B) name of the just is blessed."

4. True or False: "A false balance is abomination to the Lord."

5. Fill in the blank: "Where no _____ is, the people fall."

6. Choose A or B: "Whoso loveth instruction loveth A) the Lord B) knowledge."

7. True or False: "A man shall be commended according to his wisdom."

8. Fill in the blank: "A good man leaveth an _____ to his children's children."

9. "A _____ answer turneth away _____."
   a) harsh, people
   b) soft, wrath
   c) sweet, hostility
   d) patient, catastrophe

10. Fill in the blank: "A _____ spoken in due season, how good is it!"

Quiz 92

Proverbially Speaking, Part 4

Remember this proverb from Quiz 89: "Happy is the man that findeth wisdom"? Just think of this quiz as your continued pursuit of happiness.

1. Fill in the blanks: "Pride goeth before _____, and an haughty spirit before a _____."

2. True or False: "Better is a leaking roof, and quietness, than therewith a house full of sacrifices with strife."

3. True or False: "He that repeateth a matter separateth very friends."

4. Fill in the blank: "A friend _____ at all times."

5. Fill in the blank: "A man that hath friends must shew himself _____."

6. True or False: "Even a child is known by his doings."

7. Fill in the blank: "Train up a child in the _____ he should go: and when he is old, he will not depart from it."

8. True or False: "Open rebuke is better than secret love."

9. "The _____ flee when no man pursueth."
    a) criminals
    b) guilty
    c) horses
    d) wicked

10. Which of the following was *not* considered wonderful?
    a) the way of an eagle in the air
    b) the way of a ship in the midst of the sea
    c) the way of a man with a maid
    d) the way of bees in their hives

Quiz 93

What A Woman!

*Let's wrap up the quizzes on Proverbs by focusing on
the ideal woman of Proverbs 31. What an inspiring
way to end our journey through Proverbs!*

1. The price of a virtuous woman is far above
    a) diamonds
    b) jewels
    c) rubies
    d) silver

2. Choose A or B: The heart of her husband can safely
   A) trust B) love her.

3. True or False: "She will do him good. . .all the days of
   her life."

4. Fill in the blank: "She. . .worketh _____ with her hands."

5. What does this virtuous woman do for her family when
   she "riseth while it is yet night"?
    a) gives them meat
    b) sends the children off to school
    c) irons their clothes
    d) prays for them

6. Choose A or B: "She girdeth her loins with A) her own cloth B) strength."

7. Fill in the blank: "She stretcheth out her _____ to the poor."

8. True or False: "Her clothing is silk and purple."

9. Choose A or B: Her husband "sitteth among the A) princes B) elders of the land."

10. Fill in the blank: She shall "_____ in time to come."

Quiz 94

Ecclesiastes

Just like Proverbs, Ecclesiastes is another wisdom book of the Bible. Find out what Solomon learned about life from his experience that can make your own life more meaningful and rewarding.

1. True or False: The book of Ecclesiastes was written by a son of David.

2. Fill in the blank: According to the writer of Ecclesiastes, all is _____.

3. True or False: The writer of Ecclesiastes built himself houses and planted vineyards, but decided it was all a "vexation of spirit."

4. True or False: In the list of times in Ecclesiastes 3, it says there is a time to bury stones and a time to dig them up.

5. Two are better than one because
    a) they have a good reward for their labor.
    b) if they fall, one will lift the other up.
    c) they can keep each other warm.
    d) all of the above

6. Fill in the blank: "When thou vowest a vow unto God, defer not to pay it; for he hath no pleasure in _____."

7. True or False: "Wisdom is good with an inheritance."

8. What causes the ointment of the apothecary to give off an odor?

9. True or False: "He that diggeth a dungeon shall fall into it."

10. The whole duty of man is
    a) to work hard and provide for one's family
    b) to fear God and keep His commandments
    c) to be kind to others
    d) to contend earnestly for the faith

Ecclesiastes Fill-in-the-Blanks

Get ready for Ecclesiastes, round two. Maybe these questions on this book can help us avoid some of King Solomon's mistakes.

1. "The words of the _____, the son of David, king in Jerusalem."

2. "To every thing there is a _____, and a time to every purpose under the heaven."

3. "Better is it that thou shouldest not ____, than that thou shouldest ____ and not pay."

4. "A good name is better than precious _____."
   - a) words
   - b) ointment
   - c) stones
   - d) sentiments

5. "Anger resteth in the bosom of _____."

6. "Live _____ with the wife whom thou lovest all the days of the life."

7. "Whatsoever thy hand findeth to do, do it with thy _____."

8. "Cast thy _____ upon the waters: for thou shalt find it after many days."
   a) bread
   b) line
   c) net
   d) wish

9. "Remember now thy _____ in the days of thy youth."

10. "God shall bring every _____ into judgment."

Quiz 96

A Love Song

Love songs have been around for a long time, and this book in the Bible is one of the oldest. See how well you do at this interesting quiz.

1. According to Solomon, love is better than
   a) kisses
   b) wine
   c) gold
   d) precious ointment

2. Fill in the blanks: "We will make thee borders of _____ with studs of _____."

3. Choose A or B: "Behold, thou art fair; thou hast A) doves' B) sparkling eyes."

4. Fill in the blank: "As the lily among _____, so is my love among the daughters."

5. He brought her to the banqueting house and his _____ over her was love.
   a) cloak
   b) umbrella
   c) wish
   d) banner

6. Fill in the blank: "My beloved is _____."

7. Fill in the blank: "Thou hast _____ my heart."

8. True or False: Solomon likens his spouse to a garden enclosed.

9. "I am my beloved's, and his _____ is toward me."
   a) attention
   b) hope
   c) desire
   d) praise

10. Choose A or B: "Set me as a A) seal B) beloved one upon thine heart."

Quiz 97

Introducing Isaiah

*The first few chapters of Isaiah introduce the prophet and
tell about his call by the Lord. What do you recall
about Isaiah from these background chapters?*

1. Which of the following was not a king during Isaiah's
   prophetic ministry?
   - a) Hezekiah
   - b) Uzziah
   - c) Ahaz
   - d) Zedekiah

2. God told the sinful people, "Come now, and let us _____
   together."
   - a) walk
   - b) reason
   - c) talk
   - d) explore

3. True or False: Isaiah saw the Lord sitting upon a cloud.

4. Choose A or B: The angels Isaiah saw were A) seraphim
   B) cherubim.

5. How many wings did each angel have?

6. Who said, "Holy, holy, holy; is the Lord of hosts"?

7. Who said, "Woe is me! For I am undone"?

8. Fill in the blank: One of the angels took a live _____ and placed it on Isaiah's mouth.

9. Fill in the blank: "Whom shall I _____, and who will go for us?"

10. What did Isaiah say in response to the words in Question 9?

Quiz 98

Prophecies of the Christ

Chapters 7 and 9 of Isaiah are known for their prophecies about Christ. These questions should make you thankful for the Christ who came and purchased our salvation.

1. Fill in the blank: "Behold, a _____ shall conceive, and bear a son."

2. Fill in the blank: "And shall call his name _____."

3. True or False: "The child shall know to refuse the evil, and choose the good."

4. Fill in the blank: "For unto us a _____ is born."

5. Choose A or B: "And the A) glory of the Lord B) government shall be upon his shoulder."

6. Fill in the blank: "And his _____ shall be called Wonderful."

7. Which of the following is *not* a name for the coming Christ?
    a) Counselor
    b) Mighty God
    c) King of Nations
    d) Prince of Peace

8. Fill in the blank: "Of the _____ of his government and peace there shall be no end."

9. What king's throne was the Christ to reign upon?
    a) Hezekiah's
    b) David's
    c) Solomon's
    d) Ahab's

10. Choose A or B: "The A) zeal B) might of the Lord of hosts will perform this."

Quotable Isaiah—
Fill-in-the-Blanks

Isaiah is a long book, but it is also one of the most familiar to Bible students. How many of the missing words from the following quotations can you identify?

1. "Though your sins be as _____, they shall be as white as snow."

2. "They shall beat their _____ into plowshares."
   - a) spears
   - b) shields
   - c) plates
   - d) swords

3. "The wolf also shall dwell with the _____."

4. "And a little _____ shall lead them."

5. "He was _____ for our transgressions."

6. "With his _____ we are healed."
   - a) stripes
   - b) death
   - c) hands
   - d) cross

162

7. "All we like _____ have gone astray."

8. "_____ ye the LORD, while he may be found."

9. "For my _____ are not your _____."

10. "For as the _____ are higher than the earth, so are my ways higher than your ways."

Quiz 100

Historical Isaiah

You will need to think in historical terms in the following quiz. How many of these people, places, and events from the book of Isaiah do you recall?

1. Sennacherib was the king of
    a) Assyria
    b) Syria
    c) Damascus
    d) Babylon

2. True or False: Sennacherib took all the defenced, or walled, cities of Judah.

3. Choose A or B: Sennacherib sent A) Rabshakeh B) Eliakim to King Hezekiah.

4. Who said, "Lo, thou trusteth in the staff of this broken reed, on Egypt"?
   a) Isaiah
   b) Sennacherib
   c) Rabshakeh
   d) Hezekiah

5. Choose A or B: After the Lord dealt with Sennacherib, Sennacherib went away and dwelt at A) Nineveh B) Nod.

6. When the Lord promised Hezekiah that He would add fifteen years to Hezekiah's life, what sign did the Lord give Hezekiah?

7. Who said, "Let them take a lump of figs, and lay it for a plaister upon the boil, and he shall recover"?

8. What mistake did Hezekiah make when the king of Babylon came to visit?

9. What was the result of Hezekiah's mistake?

10. Fill in the blanks: There was _____ and _____ in the days of Hezekiah.

Quiz 101

Jeremiah the Prophet

*Jeremiah's task was to deliver a message of gloom
and doom to God's people. This quiz shows
that he was obedient to God's assignment.*

1. Jeremiah was a prophet during the reign of which of the following kings?
   a) Josiah
   b) Jehoiakim
   c) Zedekiah
   d) all of the above

2. Fill in the blanks: To Jeremiah's excuse that he was only a child, God responded, "Say not, I am a child: for thou shalt go to all that I shall send thee, and whatsoever I _____ thee thou shalt _____."

3. Choose A or B: The Lord had Jeremiah use a A) girdle B) mantle as a parable for the people.

4. Jeremiah called the Lord the _____ of Israel.
   a) hope
   b) glory
   c) deliverer
   d) salvation

5. True or False: The Lord told Jeremiah that the house of Israel was in the Lord's hand, just as clay was in the hand of the potter.

6. To whom was the Lord speaking when he said, "Ye have scattered my flock" and "behold, I will visit upon you the evil of your doings"?

7. True or False: The Lord likened His people to good and spoiled grapes.

8. Choose A or B: Jeremiah's scribe was A) Neriah B) Baruch.

9. True or False: When the Lord's words were read to the king, he cut the scroll up with a knife and burned it.

10. Fill in the blank: When Jeremiah was put in the dungeon, he sank in _____.

Quiz 102

Quotable Jeremiah

Like Isaiah in Quiz 99, Jeremiah also knew how to turn a phrase. How well can you recall Jeremiah's words and the words of the Lord in this quiz?

1. "Before I formed thee in the belly I _____ thee."
    a) watched
    b) knew
    c) called
    d) took

2. "It is not in man that walketh to _____ his steps."

3. "For I know the thoughts that I think toward you, saith the Lord, thoughts of _____."

4. "And ye shall seek me, and find me, when ye shall search for me with all your _____."

5. "I have loved thee with an _____ love."

6. "Call unto me, and I will answer thee, and show thee _____ and _____ things."

7. "Behold, that which I have built will I _____ down, and that which I have planted I will _____ up."

8. "Be not _____, O Israel: for, behold, I will _____ thee from afar off."
   a) dismayed, save
   b) impatient, feed
   c) sinful, call
   d) angry, comfort

9. "_____ be he that doeth the work of the Lord deceitfully."

10. "Leave thy fatherless children, I will preserve them alive; and let thy _____ trust in me."

The Fall of Jerusalem

*As Jeremiah predicted, Jerusalem and the nation of
Judah did eventually fall to foreign invaders.
This quiz tells how it happened.*

1. Fill in the blank: In the _____ year of Zedekiah,
   Nebuchadnezzar besieged Jerusalem.

2. True or False: All the princes of the king of Babylon came
   in and sat in the middle gate.

3. Fill in the blank: When Zedekiah and all his men of war
   saw them, they _____.

4. The Chaldean army overtook Zedekiah on the plains of
   a) Jordan
   b) Judea
   c) Jerusalem
   d) Jericho

5. True or False: The king of Assyria killed the sons of
   Zedekiah and the nobles of Judah.

6. Who said, "Take him, and look well to him, and do him
   no harm; but do unto him even as he shall say unto
   thee"?

7. Who was being referred to in question 6?
   a) Isaiah
   b) Zedekiah
   c) Jeremiah
   d) Baruch

8. True or False: The Lord told the people to stay in their land, but they wanted to go to Egypt.

9. To whom was the Lord speaking when He said, "Ye provoke me unto wrath with the works of your hands, burning incense unto other gods"?

10. Fill in the blank: "Thus Judah was carried away _____ out of his own land."

Quiz 104

A Lament

Think of the book of Lamentations as a prolonged lament over the fall of the city of Jerusalem. These questions reflect Jeremiah's sorrow and sadness over that event.

1. Fill in the blank: "How doth the city sit _____, that was full of people!"

2. Fill in the blank: "Judah is gone into _____."

3. The ways of Zion mourn because
    a) none come to the solemn feasts.
    b) her gates are desolate.
    c) she is in bitterness.
    d) all of the above

4. Choose A or B: "All her A) beauty B) hope is departed" from the daughter of Zion.

5. Why was Jerusalem despised?
    a) because garbage was rotting in the streets
    b) because the city had run out of water
    c) because the city wall had been torn down
    d) because she had sinned grievously against the Lord

6. Fill in the blank: "The LORD covered the daughter of Zion with a cloud in his _____."

7. True or False: The Lord abandoned His sanctuary.

8. Fill in the blank: It was because of the Lord's _____ that the people of Judah were not consumed.

9. Fill in the blank: "_____ is thy faithfulness."

10. Fill in the blanks: The writer of Lamentations asked the Lord to "renew our _____ as of _____."

Quiz 105

The Prophet Ezekiel

*God gave Ezekiel the task of prophesying to His people
while they were in exile in a foreign land. How much
do you recall about this famous prophet?*

1. True or False: Ezekiel was among the captives in Nineveh.

2. True or False: The spirit of the Lord entered into Ezekiel.

3. Fill in the blank: The Lord called the people of Israel a
   "_____ nation."

4. Choose A or B: Ezekiel used a A) tile B) pot portraying
   the city of Jerusalem to tell the people about the siege.

5. Ezekiel lay on his side for how many days to symbolize
   the siege of Jerusalem?
   a) 30 days
   b) 390 days
   c) 117 days
   d) 210 days

6. True or False: The Lord told Ezekiel to prophesy against
   the mountains of Israel.

7. Choose A or B: The angels Ezekiel saw were A) seraphim
   B) cherubim.

8. What is the special title by which Ezekiel is addressed by the Lord throughout the book?
   a) man of God
   b) prophet to the exiles
   c) son of man
   d) son of sorrow

9. True or False: "The soul that sinneth, it shall die."

10. True or False: When Ezekiel's wife died, the Lord told him to mourn for her for forty days.

Quiz 106

Strange Visions

Ezekiel is known for his strange visions. How much do you remember about these odd things that the Lord allowed him to see?

1. "I looked, and, behold, a _____ came out of the north."
   a) lion
   b) whirlwind
   c) beast
   d) chariot

2. True or False: The creatures came out of the midst of a great cloud with fire unfolding itself.

3. The four living creatures had the likeness of
    a) a man
    b) a monkey
    c) a bird
    d) a sheep

4. Fill in the blanks: "Every one had _____ faces, and every one had _____ wings."

5. Fill in the blank: The living creatures ran and returned as the appearance of _____.

6. True or False: Into the vision of the four creatures appeared a vision of wheels.

7. When Ezekiel saw the bones in the valley, the Lord asked him, "Can these bones _____?"
    a) jump
    b) breathe
    c) sing
    d) live

8. True or False: When Ezekiel prophesied, the bones fled.

9. Fill in the blank: "But there was no _____ in them."

10. True or False: The bones represented the house of Israel.

Quiz 107

Ezekiel on the End Times

The Lord also allowed Ezekiel to glimpse the future and see what would happen in the end times. Test your recollection of what the prophet saw with this quiz.

1. In Ezekiel's parable of the two sticks, what did the sticks represent?
   a) Babylon and Assyria
   b) Samaria and Jerusalem
   c) Judah and Israel
   d) Egypt and Ethiopia

2. Ezekiel was told to prophesy against
   a) Gog
   b) Edom
   c) Babylon
   d) Nineveh

3. Fill in the blanks: God told Ezekiel, "Now will I bring again the captivity of _____, and have mercy upon the whole house of _____."

4. In Ezekiel's vision in the twenty-fifth year of Judah's captivity, Ezekiel was set upon
   a) the temple   c) the wall of Jerusalem
   b) a high mountain   d) dry land

5. Fill in the blank: In the vision, the man had a measuring
   _____.

6. True or False: Ezekiel's vision was about the ark of the
   covenant.

7. Choose A or B: The land was to be divided by A) lots
   B) the Lord.

8. Fill in the blanks: "Ye shall have _____ balances, and a ____
   ephah, and a _____ bath."

9. True or False: A river flowed out from under the house
   (temple).

10. Fill in the blanks: "And the name of the city from that
    day shall be, The _____ is _____."

Quiz 108

Introducing Daniel

*Maybe you've heard the phrase "Dare to be a Daniel."
This quiz should refresh your memory on
who this prophet was and what he did.*

1. True or False: Daniel's Babylonian name was
   Belteshazzar.

2. Fill in the blank: "Daniel _____ in his heart that he would not defile himself with the portion of the king's meat."

3. Choose A or B: Melzar was set over Daniel and his friends by the prince of A) Babylon B) eunuchs.

4. How many days did Daniel and his friends eat the food they requested as a test?
   - a) three
   - b) seven
   - c) ten
   - d) fourteen

5. Fill in the blanks: "God gave them _____ and skill in all learning and _____."

6. When Nebuchadnezzar had his dream, whom did he call to tell him what it was?
   - a) magicians
   - b) astrologers
   - c) sorcerers
   - d) all of the above

7. True or False: The figure in Nebuchadnezzar's dream was made of glass.

8. Fill in the blanks: "Thou, O king, art a _____ of _____."

9. True or False: The image in Nebuchadnezzar's dream represented different kingdoms.

10. Fill in the blank: Because Daniel interpreted Nebuchadnezzar's dream, Nebuchadnezzar made Daniel "_____ of the governors over all the wise men of Babylon."

Quiz 109

A Fiery Furnace

There's hot, and then there's "fiery furnace" hot. What do you recall about this famous execution chamber in the book of Daniel?

1. The image Nebuchadnezzar erected on the plain or Dura was made of
   - a) wood
   - b) brass
   - c) gold
   - d) ivory

2. Fill in the blank: Any time the people heard music, they were to _____ the image.

3. Who told the king that Shadrach, Meshach, and Abednego refused to bow down and worship the image?
   - a) magicians
   - b) Chaldeans
   - c) Jews
   - d) princes

4. Who said, "If it be so, our God whom we serve is able to deliver us from the burning fiery furnace, and he will deliver us out of thine hand, O king"?

5. True or False: Nebuchadnezzar commanded that the furnace be heated three times hotter than normal.

6. Who was commanded to bind Shadrach, Meshach, and Abednego?
   - a) servants
   - b) mighty men
   - c) princes
   - d) slaves

7. True or False: The hot fire killed the people who threw Shadrach, Meshach, and Abednego into the fiery furnace.

8. Who said, "Lo, I see four men loose, walking in the midst of the fire"?

9. Fill in the blank: "The form of the fourth is like the _____ of ____."

10. True or False: Nebuchadnezzar made a decree that anyone who spoke against the God of Shadrach, Meshach, and Abednego would be hacked to pieces.

Quiz 110

The Lion's Den

This just in from Persia: "Big Cats Miss an Easy Meal."
These questions about Daniel's miraculous
escape should give you no problem.

1. Who was the king of Persia when Daniel was thrown into the lion's den?

    a) Darius
    b) Artaxerxes
    c) Shalmaneser
    d) Sennacherib

2. Choose A or B: The people who tried to find fault in Daniel were A) magicians and sorcerers B) presidents and princes.

3. True or False: The men knew they couldn't find any fault against Daniel unless it had to do with the law of Daniel's God.

4. True or False: The king was tricked into passing a law stating that no one could ask a petition of anyone but him for thirty days.

5. Fill in the blanks: The king's law was the law of the _____ and _____.

6. How many times a day did Daniel kneel and pray?
    a) one
    b) two
    c) three
    d) four

7. True or False: The king was eager to have Daniel thrown into the lion's den.

8. Who said to Daniel, "Thy God whom thou servest continually, he will deliver thee"?

9. Who did God send to shut the lions' mouths?

10. True or False: The king had the men who accused Daniel thrown into the lion's den.

Daniel on the End Times

*Just as God allowed Ezekiel to glimpse the future
(see Quiz 107), He gave this same ability
to Daniel. What did Daniel see?*

1. Daniel had a vision about four beasts. Which one of the following was *not* in the vision?
   a) bear
   b) lion
   c) leopard
   d) serpent

2. Fill in the blank: Daniel saw a throne upon which sat the _____ of days.

3. Fill in the blank: The Son of man was given _____ dominion.

4. True or False: The ten horns on the fourth beast represented ten kings.

5. When Daniel had the vision of the ram and goat, who was sent to explain it to him?
   a) Gabriel
   b) Michael
   c) a prophet
   d) a priest

6. True or False: The vision caused Daniel to celebrate and praise the Lord.

7. Choose A or B: A) Gabriel B) Michael was the great prince who stood for Daniel's people.

8. Fill in the blank: Daniel was told to "shut up the words" and "_____ the book, even to the time of the end."

9. True or False: The time was to be for "a time, times, and an half."

10. Fill in the blank: "_____ is he that waiteth."

Quiz 112

Hosea's Sad Story

Hosea's marriage was not a bed of roses, but God used it to get across His message to His people. What else do you remember about this prophet?

1. Hosea prophesied during which king's reign?
    a) Uzziah
    b) Jotham
    c) Hezekiah
    d) all of the above

2. Choose A or B: Hosea's wife was A) Zipporah B) Gomer.

3. How many children did Hosea have?

4. Who named Hosea's children?
   a) Gomer
   b) Hosea
   c) Hosea's mother
   d) God

5. Which of the following names meant "I will no more have mercy upon the house of Israel"?
   a) Jezreel
   b) Loruhamah
   c) Lo-ammi
   d) Diblaim

6. True or False: When Hosea's wife was unfaithful to him, the Lord told Hosea to treat her like an adulteress and have her stoned.

7. True or False: The Lord used Hosea's situation as a parallel to the way Israel treated the Lord.

8. Fill in the blank: "When Israel was a child, then I loved him, and called my son out of _____."

9. True or False: The Lord said He would heal Israel's backslidings and love them freely.

10. Fill in the blank: "For the ways of the LORD are _____, and the just shall walk in them."

Quiz 113

The Prophet Joel

Joel had a lot to say about the Day of the Lord.
These questions show what that future day will be like.

1. True or False: The Day of the Lord would be a day of cheerfulness and light.

2. Fill in the blanks: In the day of the Lord, the earth shall _____ and the heavens shall _____.

3. "Rend your _____, and not your garments."
    a) sins
    b) heart
    c) thoughts
    d) attitudes

4. Choose A or B: "And it shall come to pass afterward, that I will pour out my A) spirit B) love upon all flesh."

5. Fill in the blank: "Your sons and your daughters shall _____."

6. What would the old men do in the day spoken of by Joel?
    a) dream dreams
    b) counsel the young
    c) live bountifully
    d) rest from their work

7. Choose A or B: The young men shall A) see visions B) dream dreams.

8. Fill in the blank: "Whosoever shall call on the name of the LORD shall be _____."

9. True or False: In that day God will dwell in Zion.

10. Choose A or B: "Then shall Jerusalem be holy, and there shall no A) pilgrims B) strangers pass through her any more."

Quiz 114

Amos and Obadiah

Both Amos and Obadiah were prophets, but that's about all they had in common. Your challenge is to sort them out in this quiz.

1. Before he was a prophet, Amos was a
    a) carpenter
    b) stone mason
    c) leather worker
    d) herdsman

2. True or False: Amos prophesied in the days of King Uzziah.

3. Which of the following places did Amos *not* prophesy against?
   a) Damascus
   b) Tyrus
   c) Edom
   d) Nineveh

4. Fill in the blank: "Can two walk together, except they be _____?"

5. True or False: The Lord said His people would rebuild their destroyed cities.

6. Against whom did Obadiah prophesy?

7. Fill in the blanks: "Behold, I have made thee small among the _____: thou art greatly _____."

8. Fill in the blank: "For thy _____ against thy brother. . . thou shalt be cut off for ever."

9. True or False: Obadiah prophesied that the house of Jacob would be a fire consuming the stubble of the house of Isaac.

10. Fill in the blank: "And the kingdom shall be the _____."

Jonah's Tale

*There's more to the prophet Jonah than the big fish.
Show how much else you know about him
by answering these questions correctly.*

1. The Lord wanted Jonah to go to prophesy against
    a) Jerusalem
    b) Nineveh
    c) Rome
    d) Antioch

2. True or False: Jonah tried to flee to Tarshish.

3. How did the mariners decide who was causing the
   problem aboard the ship?

4. Whose idea was it to throw Jonah into the sea?

5. Fill in the blank: "Now the LORD had _____ a great fish to
   swallow up Jonah."

6. How long was Jonah in the belly of the fish?
    a) one day and two nights
    b) part of one day
    c) eight hours
    d) three days and three nights

7. How did Jonah get out of the belly of the fish?

8. When the people to whom he prophesied repented, Jonah was
   a) angry
   b) glad
   c) relieved
   d) very happy

9. Who said, "It is better for me to die than to live"?

10. True or False: Jonah sat on the east side of the city in a booth.

Quiz 116

Micah's Ministry

*Micah is known as a minor prophet, but there
was nothing minor about his ministry. See how
much you can recall about his life and times.*

1. Micah prophesied during the reign of
   a) King David   c) King Hezekiah
   b) King Josiah   d) King Solomon

2. To what cities did Micah prophesy?

3. Choose A or B: The Lord will come down and "tread upon the A) high B) low places of the earth."

4. "All the _____ _____ thereof shall be beaten to pieces."
   a) sharp swords
   b) graven images
   c) sinful people
   d) dumb idols

5. Choose A or B: "Woe to them that devise A) iniquity B) plots."

6. Fill in the blank: "But in the last days it shall come to pass, that the mountain of the house of the LORD shall be _____."

7. True or False: The Lord said he would make of her "that was cast far off a strong nation."

8. "But thou, _____ Ephratah. . .out of thee shall he come forth unto me that is to be _____ in Israel."
   a) Samaria, commander
   b) Nazareth, sorrowful
   c) Capernaum, sovereign
   d) Bethlehem, ruler

9. True or False: The Lord told His people to testify against Him.

10. Fill in the blank: "Who is a God like unto thee, that _____ iniquity. . .because he delighteth in mercy."

Quiz 117

Nahum and Habakkuk

*Habakkuk follows Nahum in the Old Testament.
That's about the only reason we can give you for
putting these two prophets together in this quiz.
But you're smart enough to sort them out.*

1. To whom did Nahum prophesy?
   a) Nineveh
   b) Babylon
   c) Egypt
   d) Persepolis

2. Fill in the blank: "The LORD is _____ to anger, and great
   in power."

3. Choose A or B: "The LORD is good, a strong hold in the
   day of A) wrath B) trouble."

4. Choose A or B: "The LORD hath given a
   A) commandment B) covenant concerning thee."

5. Who did the Lord have in mind when he said, "I am
   against thee."
   a) the citizens of Nineveh   c) the residents of Judah
   b) all sinful people   d) the priests in Jerusalem

6. Who said, "O LORD, how long shall I cry, and thou wilt
   not hear!"
   a) Nahum   c) Habakkuk
   b) Amos   d) Zephaniah

7. Fill in the blank: "For, lo, I raise up the _____, that bitter and hasty nation."

8. Fill in the blank: "The just shall live by his _____."

9. Choose A or B: "Woe unto him that. . .stablisheth a city by A) blood B) iniquity!"

10. Fill in the blank: "The LORD God is my strength, and he will make my feet like _____ feet, and he will make me to walk upon mine high places."

Quiz 118

Zephaniah and Haggai

In this case, Zephaniah comes before Haggai in the Old Testament (see our rationale for Quiz 117), so that's why we put these two prophets together in the same quiz. If you don't see the humor in this, you can get even by doing a slam dunk on these questions.

1. Zephaniah prophesied during the rule of what king?
   a) King Jeroboam
   b) King Josiah
   c) King Ahab
   d) King Hezekiah

2. Fill in the blank: Zephaniah prophesied about the day of
_____.

3. True or False: Zephaniah prophesied that this day would
be a day of "the trumpet and alarm."

4. Choose A or B: "Her prophets are A) righteous and
faithful B) light and treacherous persons."

5. Fill in the blank: "The LORD thy God. . .will joy over thee
with _____."

6. True or False: Haggai prophesied during the reign of King
Artaxerxes.

7. Who said, "The time is not come, the time that the LORD's
house should be built"?

8. Fill in the blanks: "The glory of this _____ house shall be
greater than of the _____."

9. True or False: When Haggai prophesied, Zerubbabel was
governor of Judah.

10. Who was the Lord referring to when He said, "I. . .will
make thee as a signet: for I have chosen thee."
    a) King Darius
    b) the prophet Haggai
    c) Zerubbabel
    d) Nehemiah

Quiz 119

The Prophet Zechariah

Zechariah urged the people of Judah to complete the rebuilding of the temple after their return from exile in a foreign land. See how much you recall about his life and ministry.

1. Who was the king of Persia when the word of the Lord came to Zechariah?
   - a) Ahasuerus
   - b) Artaxerxes
   - c) Nebuchadnezzar I
   - d) Darius

2. Fill in the blanks: "_____ ye unto me, saith the LORD of hosts, and I will _____ unto you."

3. Choose A or B: "The LORD of hosts thought to do unto us, according to our ways, and according to our A) thoughts B) doings, so hath he dealt with us."

4. Fill in the blank: Zechariah had a vision of a man on a red _____.

5. Zechariah had a vision of a man with a _____ _____ in his hand.
   - a) long spear
   - b) measuring line
   - c) small shield
   - d) sledge hammer

6. Fill in the blank: "Behold, I will bring forth my servant the _____."

7. True or False: The Lord said the people's hearts were like a flint rock.

8. Choose A or B: "Thus saith the LORD of hosts; I was jealous for Zion with great jealousy, and I was jealous for her with great A) love B) fury."

9. True or False: "In that day shall there be one LORD, and his name one."

10. Fill in the blank: "Every pot in Jerusalem and in Judah shall be _____ unto the LORD."

Quiz 120

The Last Book of the Old Testament

This prophet concludes the Old Testament by calling on God's people to be more committed to Him. Let that be his message to you as you answer the questions on this quiz.

1. To whom did Malachi prophesy?
    a) Israel   c) Egypt
    b) Judah   d) Moab

2. True or False: The Lord said he hated Jacob and loved Esau.

3. Fill in the blank: "Ye offer _____ bread upon mine altar."

4. True or False: The Lord said the people should offer to their governor the same sacrifices they offered Him and see if the governor would be pleased with them.

5. Fill in the blank: "Behold, I will send my _____, and he shall prepare the way before me."

6. Choose A or B: The Lord shall come A) patiently B) suddenly to His temple.

7. How had the people "robbed" God?
   a) by stealing gold from the temple
   b) by cheating people in their buying and selling
   c) by failing to give their tithes and offerings
   d) by offering sick animals as sacrifices

8. Fill in the blank: "Bring ye all the _____ into the store-house."

9. Choose A or B: The Sun of righteousness [shall] arise with A) healing B) glory in his wings.

10. Who did the Lord say He would send "before the coming of the great and dreadful day of the LORD"?
    a) Elijah
    b) Nathan
    c) Elisha
    d) Micah

Quiz 121

One Amazing Pregnancy

Jesus was miraculously conceived in the womb of Mary by the Holy Spirit. These questions test your recollection of this amazing event.

1. Who told Jesus' mother that she would give birth to "a son. . . JESUS"?
   a) the angel Gabriel
   b) the Holy Ghost
   c) wise men from the east
   d) Zacharias the priest

2. How does the Bible describe Mary to assure that her pregnancy was miraculous?

3. Fill in the blank: "Fear not, Mary: for thou hast found _____ with God."

4. Who was Mary's espoused husband?

5. How did Mary's husband plan to "put her away" [divorce her] when he learned of her pregnancy?
   a) angrily
   b) painfully
   c) privily
   d) quickly

6. How did an angel speak to Mary's husband to change his divorce plans?

7. In what city was Mary living when she learned of her role in Jesus' birth?
   a) Bethlehem   c) Jerusalem
   b) Emmaus   d) Nazareth

8. True or False: Mary had no questions about the news of her pregnancy.

9. What relative did the expectant Mary visit for three months?

10. Fill in the blanks: "Thou shalt call his name JESUS: for he shall save his people from _____ _____."

Quiz 122

A Genealogy

Both Matthew and Luke contain genealogies of the human family line of Jesus. Your challenge is to sort them out in this quiz.

1. Fill in the blank: "The book of the generation of Jesus Christ, the son of _____."

196

2. To what man does Matthew trace Jesus' genealogy?

3. To what man does Luke trace Jesus' genealogy?

4. How many generations are in the three groupings Matthew describes?
    a) seven   c) fourteen
    b) ten   d) twenty

5. True or False: Deborah, the Old Testament judge, is listed in Jesus' genealogy.

6. Which of the twelve sons of Jacob was part of Jesus' lineage?
    a) Dan   c) Naphtali
    b) Judah   d) Reuben

7. What murdered soldier, husband of Bathsheba, is mentioned in Matthew's genealogy?

8. What prominent Old Testament woman is named in Matthew's genealogy?
    a) Delilah   c) Hannah
    b) Esther   d) Ruth

9. True or False: Noah, or Noe, is mentioned in Luke's genealogy of Jesus.

10. What child of Adam and Eve became part of the line of Christ?

Quiz 123

Special Delivery

These questions are about the birth of Jesus.
We hear this old, wonderful story often at Christmastime.
Go for a slam dunk on this quiz.

1. Who was the Caesar who decreed a tax upon the whole world?

2. Where did Joseph travel with Mary to be taxed?
   a) Bethlehem
   b) Damascus
   c) Jerusalem
   d) Cairo

3. How did the shepherds first react when the angels appeared and the glory of the Lord shone around them?

4. Who said, "I bring you good tidings of great joy"?
   a) an angel
   b) a member of the heavenly host
   c) a shepherd
   d) a wise man

5. Choose A or B: The birth of the Saviour would be tidings of great joy to A) Jewish B) all people.

6. Fill in the blank: Mary purified herself "according to the law of _____."

7. Where did Simeon and Anna see Jesus?
   a) in Nazareth
   b) in the manger
   c) in the temple at Jerusalem
   d) on the road to Damascus

8. How were the wise men warned not to return to Herod?

9. Because of the danger from Herod, Joseph took Mary and Jesus to what country?

10. After what event was Joseph told to return with Mary and Jesus to the land of Israel?

Quiz 124

The Boyhood of Christ

Luke is the only Gospel writer that tells us anything about Jesus' growing-up years. This quiz should prepare you for the beginning of His ministry.

1. How often did Jesus' parents go to Jerusalem?

2. How old was Jesus when He talked with the doctors in the temple?
   a) six years old   c) twelve years old
   b) eight years old   d) thirty years old

3. How long did Jesus' parents travel without Him before they turned back?

4. How many days did Jesus' parents search for Jesus?

5. How did the doctors of the temple react upon hearing the young Jesus?
   a) they were angry
   b) they were astonished
   c) they were sorrowful
   d) they were without understanding

6. How did Jesus reply when His parents found him?
   a) "Fear not; I am the first and the last"
   b) "I must be about my Father's business"
   c) "It is finished"
   d) "What have I to do with thee? mine hour is not yet come."

7. Fill in the blank: Jesus grew up in the town of _____.

8. True or False: After the events in the temple, Jesus was no longer subject to his parents.

9. Where did Mary keep all of the sayings of Jesus?

10. Fill in the blanks: "Jesus increased in wisdom and stature, and in favour with _____ and _____."

Quiz 125

John the Baptist

John the Baptist prepared people for the beginning of Jesus'
ministry. These questions should help you appreciate John's
humility and contribution to the cause of the gospel.

1. Who were the parents of John the Baptist?
   - a) Ananias and Sapphira
   - c) Cleophas and Mary
   - b) Aquila and Priscilla
   - d) Zacharias and Elisabeth

2. Fill in the blank: "He shall go before him in the spirit and
   power of Elias (Elijah). . .to make ready a people_____
   for the Lord."

3. Choose A or B: John had the same name as A) his grandfather B) none of his relatives.

4. How did John's father tell others his newborn son's name?

5. In speaking of Jesus (the one who would come after),
   what did John say he was unworthy to do?
   - a) eat at the same table
     as Jesus
   - c) unloose the
     shoes of Jesus
   - b) place a fan in His hand
   - d) wear the robe of Jesus

6. Fill in the blank: "Repent ye: for the kingdom of _____
   is at hand."

7. John the Baptist ate locusts and A) goat's milk B) wild honey.

8. What did John the Baptist say when he saw the Pharisees and Sadducees?
    a) "I know thy rebellion, and thy stiff neck."
    b) "O generation of vipers."
    c) "They will not endure sound doctrine."
    d) "Your house is left unto you desolate."

9. What event was being celebrated when Herod rashly promised to give the daughter of Herodias anything she asked?

10. Who buried the body of John the Baptist?

Quiz 126

Jesus' Ministry Begins

When the time was right in accordance with God's plan, Jesus launched His public ministry. Think of this quiz as the eager preparation for an exciting journey. Jesus' life and ministry will be the focus of the next twenty-five quizzes.

1. Fill in the blank: "Behold the Lamb of God, which taketh away the _____ of the world."

2. What form did the Spirit take when Jesus came out of the water after being baptized?

3. At about what age was Jesus baptized?

4. At the baptism of Jesus, what did the voice from heaven say?
    a) "Behold, the kingdom of heaven is at hand."
    b) "Can any good thing come out of Nazareth?"
    c) "Prepare ye the way of the Lord, make his paths straight."
    d) "This is my beloved Son, in whom I am well pleased."

5. How long did Jesus fast in the desert?

6. When did the devil say to Jesus, "Command this stone that it be made bread"?

7. Choose A or B: During the temptation, the phrase "For it is written" was spoken by A) Jesus alone B) both Jesus and the devil.

8. Fill in the blank: "Now after that John was put in prison, Jesus came into Galilee, preaching the _____ of the kingdom of God."

9. How did the passage begin from Esaias (Isaiah) that Jesus read in the synagogue?
    a) "All things are possible with God."
    b) "Give and it shall be given to you."
    c) "Seek and save the lost."
    d) "The Spirit of the Lord is upon me."

10. When Jesus finished speaking to those in the synagogue in Nazareth, what was His listeners' reaction?
    a) They glorified His name.
    b) They fell back and bowed down before Him.
    c) They straightway forgot His teachings.
    d) They were filled with wrath.

Quiz 127

The Sermon on the Mount

How well do you recall Jesus' famous teachings to
His followers in Matthew 5–7? This quiz should
serve as a good review of this famous sermon.

1. What blessing does Jesus give to the poor in spirit?

2. What blessing does Jesus give to the meek?

3, What blessing shall the pure in heart receive?
    a) they shall be called children of God
    b) they shall be comforted
    c) they shall become the salt of the earth
    d) they shall see God

4. Choose A or B: As for the law and the prophets, Jesus
   came to A) destroy them B) fulfill them.

5. Fill in the blank: "But I say unto you, _____ your enemies."

6. What should a person do when giving alms?
    a) also lay up treasures on earth
    b) do so in secret
    c) never give silver or gold
    d) sound a trumpet to glorify God

7. Fill in the blank: "For where your treasure is, there will
   your _____ be also."

8. What plant did Jesus say was arrayed with greater splendor than Solomon?

9. Choose A or B: "Strait is the gate, and A) broad B) narrow is the way, which leadeth unto life."

10. According to Jesus' warning, how might false prophets come?
   a) as a good tree with bad fruit
   b) as dry clouds with a whirlwind
   c) as fowls of the air
   d) as wolves in sheep's clothing

Quiz 128

Be Healed!
Part 1

Jesus healed many people who suffered from diseases and physical problems or disabilities. How many of these healing events can you identify?

1. The man sick of the palsy who was let down through the roof was carried by how many men?

2. Why did the men bearing the man sick with palsy let him down to Jesus through the roof?

3. During the healing of the man let down through the roof,
who said, "Who can forgive sins but God only?"
   a) Jesus
   b) man let through the roof
   c) scribes
   d) those who carried the man

4. Who asked Jesus to heal the centurion's servant?

5. True or False: The centurion felt unworthy for Jesus to
enter his house to heal his sick servant.

6. Fill in the blank: The centurion with the sick servant said,
"For I also am a man set under _____."

7. True or False: Only in Israel did Jesus find faith greater
than that of the centurion.

8. Jairus, the man whose little daughter Jesus raised from the
dead, held what leadership position?
   a) centurion   c) chief tax collector
   b) a Samaritan elder   d) a ruler of the synagogue

9. What did Jairus ask Jesus to do for his little daughter?
   a) anoint her with oil
   b) lay hands on her
   c) pray over her
   d) see the clothes she had made

10. How did the people react when Jesus said that Jarius's
daughter was not dead but sleeping?

Quiz 129

Be Healed!
Part 2

Jesus' healing ministry was so extensive that it takes two quizzes to cover it. See how well you do on these questions.

1. True or False: At Decapolis Jesus healed a man of his deafness but left his speech impediment as a thorn in his flesh so he would not be exalted.

2. What question about sin did Jesus' disciples ask when they saw the man blind from birth?

3. Fill in the blank: Before healing the man born blind, Jesus said, "I am the _____ of the world."

4. Jesus told the man born blind to wash in what body of water?
   a) Jordan River   c) Sea of Galilee
   b) pool of Siloam   d) Sheep Pool

5. What did the father of the boy with a destructive spirit say when Jesus told him that all things are possible to him who believes?
   a) "I am strong in faith, trusting God."
   b) "I believe; help thou mine unbelief."
   c) "Shall my unbelief make the power of God without effect?"
   d) "Without signs and wonders, how shall I believe?"

6. Fill in the blanks: When His disciples asked why they could not cast the destructive spirit out of the boy, Jesus said, "This kind can come forth by nothing, but by _____ and _____."

7. What question did Jesus ask before healing the man with dropsy on the Sabbath day?

8. What did the ten lepers do when they saw Jesus?
   a) broke the chains with which they were bound
   b) fell at this feet
   c) rushed to touch the helm of his garment
   d) stood afar off

9. What did Jesus tell the ten lepers to do after their healing?

10. How many of the ten lepers returned to thank Jesus for their healing?

Quiz 130

Parables of Jesus

The parables of Jesus set Him apart from many teachers of His day. See how many of His parables you can recall in this quiz.

1. What truth did Jesus illustrate with the parable of the wise and foolish builders?
   a) Foolish people do not listen to His words.
   b) Life is filled with swift transitions.

c) Rain falls on both the just and the unjust.
d) Wise people do what He says.

2. In the parable of the seeds and soils, what happened to the seeds that fell by the way side?

3. Where did the seeds fall, only to be scorched by the sun?

4. Choose A or B: Jesus explained the parable of the seeds and soils to A) all of the listeners B) His disciples alone.

5. Jesus likens those deceived by riches to which seeds?
   a) those that fell among thorns
   b) those that fell on the wayside
   c) those that grew and brought forth a hundredfold
   d) those without roots

6. When were the wheat and tares separated?
   a) when they were seeds
   b) as soon as they sprouted
   c) at the harvest
   d) never

7. What did the man sell to buy the pearl of great price?

8. What question does the parable of the Good Samaritan answer?

9. Fill in the blank: The parable of the Good Samaritan took place along the road between Jerusalem and _____.

10. True or False: The Good Samaritan stayed with the injured man until he was fully recovered.

Quiz 131

More Parables of Jesus

We couldn't squeeze all of Jesus' parables into Quiz 130, so here are some more for your attention. This is your chance to show you are a real student of His parables.

1. Fill in the blanks: The rich man with plentiful crops said to himself, "Take thine ease, _____, _____, and be _____."

2. The rich man who built more barns did not consider that
    a) his servants would rise up against him
    b) his soul would be required of him
    c) rain and wind would cause it to fall
    d) plentiful crops would be followed by seven years of famine

3. After finding the lost sheep, how did the man return it home?

4. To what does Jesus compare the lost coin?
    a) a lost child that asks his father for forgiveness
    b) a lost sheep that returns to the flock
    c) a man who has wealth but hides it
    d) one sinner who repents

5. In the parable of the wasteful (prodigal) son, what disaster came upon the far country where he journeyed?

6. What animals did the prodigal son feed after he spent his money?

7. Who was angry at the prodigal son's return?

8. Choose A or B: In the parable of the talents, the servant who hid his Lord's money was the one with the A) most talents B) fewest talents.

9. To whom did Jesus direct the parable of the Pharisee and the publican who prayed in the temple?
    a) those who gave only out of their abundance
    b) those who had extorted money
    c) those who trusted in their own righteousness
    d) those who committed adultery

10. True or False: As the publican prayed, he looked up unto heaven.

Quiz 132

Jesus Says, "I Am"

Jesus used the expression "I am" a lot. What did He mean by this expression? Find out by answering these questions.

1. What phrase completes Jesus' statement beginning "I am meek. . ."?

2. When asked directly "Whom say ye that I am?" how did Peter reply?

3. How does Jesus' promise "I am with you always," end?
    a) "and My peace I leave with you."
    b) "even unto the end of the world"
    c) "for where I go you cannot come"
    d) "until we drink together in my Father's kingdom"

4. Fill in the blank: "I am the light of the world: he that followeth me shall not walk in darkness, but shall have the light of _____."

5. How did Jesus reply when his critics said that He was under fifty years old and could not have seen Abraham?

6. In speaking of sheep, how did Jesus describe Himself?
    a) "I am come that they might have life"
    b) "I am the door of the sheep"
    c) "I am the good shepherd"
    d) all of the above

7. True or False: Jesus said, "I am the resurrection, and the life" while speaking to Martha about her brother Lazarus who had died.

8. After saying, "I am the way, the truth, and the life," how many ways did Jesus list that a man could come to the Father?

9. After saying, "I am the vine," how did Jesus describe His Father?
    a) as good ground
    b) as the husbandman
    c) as the sower of fertile seed
    d) as winds and water

10. Fill in the blank: Jesus said, "I am the vine, ye are the _____."

Quiz 133

Miracles of Jesus

*Healing miracles weren't the only spectacular
works that Jesus performed. See how well
you remember these miraculous events.*

1. At the marriage feast in Cana of Galilee, to whom did
   Jesus say, "Mine hour is not yet come"?
   - a) His disciples
   - b) His mother
   - c) the bridegroom
   - d) the governor of the feast

2. Before the miracle of the filling of the fishnets, why did
   Jesus enter the boat and ask Peter to thrust a little way
   from the land?

3. After catching a great multitude of fish, what did Simon
   Peter say?
   - a) "Can any man forbid that we eat this food?"
   - b) "Depart from me; for I am a sinful man."
   - c) "The Gentiles shall hear the word of the Gospel."
   - d) "Thou art the Son of God."

4. Fill in the blank: After seeing the son of the widow of Nain
   raised from the dead, the people said, "A great _____ is
   risen up among us."

5. Before Jesus calmed the sea, what was He doing?

6. What did Jesus say to calm the sea?

213

7. Fill in the blank: "What manner of man is this, that even the _____ and the sea obey him!"

8. True or False: The five thousand were fed with five loaves and two fish.

9. Who found the boy with the loaves and fishes?
   a) a shepherd
   b) Andrew
   c) Jesus
   d) Simon Peter

10. How many baskets of food were left over after the feeding of the five thousand?

Quiz 134

More Miracles of Jesus

This quiz continues the miracles of Jesus from Quiz 133. These wonders should impress you with His power, just as people of His time were amazed at His actions.

1. After Jesus sent the multitude away and the disciples crossed by ship to the other side without Jesus, what did they see in the fourth watch of the night?

2. True or False: The same number of loaves and fish were used to feed the four thousand as the five thousand.

3. Where did Jesus say Simon would find a coin to pay the tribute money in Capernaum?

4. Fill in the blanks: The names of Lazarus's two sisters were Mary and _____.

5. When Jesus heard that Lazarus was sick, when did Jesus leave to be with him?
     a) after hearing that Lazarus was dead
     b) after two days
     c) immediately
     d) the next morning

6. Fill in the blank: When Thomas learned Jesus was going to the home of Lazarus, he said, "Let us also go, that we may _____ with him."

7. What city was Bethany near?

8. When Jesus arrived at the tomb, how long had Lazarus been dead?

9. Choose A or B: During the arrest of Jesus, Simon Peter cut off the A) left B) right ear of Malchus.

10. After Jesus appeared along the seashore following His resurrection, how many fish were found in the net when it was pulled ashore?
     a) none
     b) an hundred and fifty and three
     c) seven times seventy
     d) a great multitude

Jesus Prays

Prayer was also a major part of Jesus' life and ministry. See how many of these questions on His prayer life you can answer.

1. What food is mentioned in the Lord's model prayer from the Sermon on the Mount?

2. Fill in the blank: "For thine is the kingdom, and the power, and the _____, for ever. Amen."

3. Who were the three disciples whom Jesus took with Him when He prayed in the Garden of Gethsemane?

4. How many times did Jesus pray in the Garden of Gethsemane?

5. When Jesus prayed in the Garden, what statement immediately follows the words, "take away this cup from me"?
   a) "Behold, the Son of man is betrayed into the hands of sinners."
   b) "But for this cause came I unto this hour."
   c) "Nevertheless not what I will, but what thou wilt."
   d) "The spirit truly is ready, but the flesh is weak."

6. What were the disciples doing as Jesus prayed in the Garden?
   a) building a memorial   c) casting stones
   b) asking who would   d) sleeping
      be greatest

7. True or False: Jesus prayed for others but never for Himself.

8. Choose A or B: When Jesus prayed for His disciples, He asked that God would A) take them out of the world B) keep them from the evil.

9. Fill in the blanks: "As thou hast _____ me into the world, even so have I also _____ them into the world."

10. When Jesus prayed for all His disciples, what did He ask that they be?
    a) an example to the brokenhearted
    b) a perfect master of His Father's word
    c) seed that grow out of season
    d) one, as He and the Father are one

Quiz 136

Teachings of Jesus

The common people were impressed with the teachings of Jesus. This quiz measures how much you remember about what He taught.

1. Because they would not repent, Jesus compared the cities of Chorazin and Bethsaida to what other two cites?
    a) Babel and Nineveh   c) Sodom and Gomorrah
    b) Rome and Antioch   d) Tyre and Sidon

2. In His sermon on love, Jesus says, "Bless them that curse you," and do what for them "that despitefully use you"?

3. Why does Jesus tell His listeners to take His yoke upon them?
   a) because believers must be led by the yoke of the Spirit
   b) because His yoke is light
   c) because they should not be yoked with unbelievers
   d) because they will find rest for their souls

4. What expression completes this sentence: "Love your enemies. . ."?
   a) as a sign to follow them that believe.
   b) because you will gain a hundredfold.
   c) do good to them which hate you.
   d) for mercy is greater than sacrifice.

5. Who does Jesus say also love those who love them, do good to those who do good to them, and lend and hope to receive?

6. True or False: Although disciples of Jesus should ask, seek, and knock, Jesus says that they should not expect their requests to be answered.

7. Fill in the blanks: "For the _____ of God is he which cometh down from heaven, and giveth life unto the world. Then said they unto him, Lord, evermore give us this _____. And Jesus said unto them, I am the _____ of life."

8. Fill in the blank: "As the Father hath _____ me, so have I _____ you."

9. Choose A or B: Jesus' commandment is that His disciples A) love B) teach one another.

10. According to Jesus, the greatest love is that a man does what?

Quiz 137

More Teachings of Jesus

This quiz also focuses on the teachings of Jesus. Test your knowledge about His teachings with these additional questions.

1. True or False: Jesus said, "[A] house divided against itself shall not stand" in answer to a question about a civil war between the Jews and Samaritans.

2. How does Jesus answer the question, "When saw we thee a stranger, and took thee in? Or naked, and clothed thee?"

3. What did Jesus say is the first commandment?

4. Fill in the blank: In reading from the book of Esaias [Isaiah], Jesus said He had been sent to preach the gospel to the poor and deliverance to the _____.

5. How does Jesus say that words "spoken in the ear in closets" will be heard?
   - a) as a memorial to evil doers
   - b) proclaimed upon the housetops
   - c) shall be judged in the last days
   - d) viewed in full and bright light

6. Who said, "For God so loved the world, that he gave his only begotten Son"?
   - a) Jesus
   - b) John the Apostle
   - c) John the Baptist
   - d) Nicodemus

7. When the light (Jesus) came into the world, why did men love darkness rather than light?

8. Fill in the blanks: "God is a _____: and they that worship him must worship him in _____ and in truth."

9. Fill in the blank: "Herein is my Father glorified, that ye bear much _____; so shall ye be my disciples."

10. To be friends of Jesus, what must believers do?
    a) Be wise in choice of companions.
    b) Call the poor, the maimed, the lame, and the blind to share a meal.
    c) Do whatever He commands.
    d) Hate His enemies.

Quiz 138

The Twelve Disciples

What do you remember about the twelve disciples whom Jesus selected? This review should make you grateful that He didn't choose more than twelve!

1. What was the profession of Simon Peter?
    a) carpenter   c) tax collector
    b) fisherman   d) tentmaker

2. Fill in the blank: "Thou art Simon the son of Jona: thou shalt be called _____, which is by interpretation, A stone."

3. Andrew was the brother of which one of the twelve disciples?
    a) James
    b) John
    c) Peter
    d) Simon Zelotes

4. Which disciples were known as "The sons of thunder"?
    a) Judas (not Iscariot) and Simon the Zealot
    b) the sons of Alphaeus
    c) the sons of Zebedee
    d) two disciples whom Jesus rejected as apostles

5. The phrase "the disciple whom Jesus loved" appears in which Gospel?

6. Why did the Pharisees murmur when Jesus ate a meal with Matthew (Levi)?

7. After seeing Jesus raised and touching the print of the nails in His hands, what did Thomas say?

8. Which of the twelve disciples carried the money bag?

9. Which of the twelve disciples used a sword to defend Jesus on the night of His arrest?

10. True or False: Bartholomew was present when Jesus was transfigured on the high mountain.

Jesus on Money

Jesus had a lot to say about money and earthly possessions. How much of His teachings on this subject do you remember?

1. Where can a treasure be put so that moth and rust does not corrupt it, and thieves cannot steal it?

2. Why does Jesus say a man cannot serve God and mammon (material wealth)?
    a) He will be a hypocrite with a sad countenance.
    b) He will hate the one and love the other.
    c) He hides his wealth to preserve it.
    d) He will spoil those of his household.

3. Fill in the blanks: "For what is a man profited, if he shall gain the _____ _____, and lose his own soul?"

4. Rather than seeking food, drink, and clothing, what should believers seek first?

5. Fill in the blank: The poor widow put _____ mites in the temple treasury.

6. Why did Jesus say the poor widow had given more than the rich people?
    a) Scribes and Pharisees had devoured her house.
    b) She had gone to the moneychangers for coins without Caesar's image.

c) Their hearts were not right, but her heart was right.

d) They gave of their abundance, but she gave all she had.

7. The moneychangers had made the temple a den of thieves, but it should have been called what kind of house by all nations?

8. What animal did Jesus use to illustrate the difficulty of a rich man entering the kingdom of God?
   a) camel
   b) sheep
   c) raven
   d) wolf

9. True or False: The just man who invites the poor, maimed, lame, and blind to dinner will receive recompense at the resurrection.

10. After the rich ruler said he had obeyed all of the commands from his youth up, what did Jesus tell him to do?

Quiz 140

Jesus and the Pharisees

Who were the Pharisees, and what did they have against Jesus? Find out by answering these questions.

1. How did Jesus reply when the Pharisees asked why He was eating with publicans and sinners?

2. How did Jesus reply when asked why His disciples did not fast, but the Pharisees often fasted?

3. When the chief priests and elders asked about His authority for doing the things He did, how did Jesus respond?

    a) by asking a question about the baptism of John the Baptist

    b) by ignoring the question

    c) by quoting from the Law and the prophets

    d) by talking about bread from heaven

4. True or False: When Jesus talked about the stone that the builders rejected, the Pharisees were not aware He was speaking of them.

5. When Jesus preached "Woe unto you, scribes and Pharisees, hypocrites," how did He use a gnat and a camel to illustrate His point?

6. Why did the scribes and Pharisees watch Jesus?

    a) to find an accusation against Him

    b) to identify his disciples and bring them before Pilate

    c) to learn how He performed miracles

    d) to see if He was paying the temple tax

7. True or False: Jesus refused to eat with the Pharisees.

8. What was "the leaven of the Pharisees"?

    a) hypocrisy   c) marriage questions

    b) manna from heaven   d) the old law

9. True or False: Nicodemus, the ruler of the Jews, who came to see Jesus by night, was a Pharisee.

10. Why did some Pharisees object when Jesus healed the blind man by making clay, putting it in his eyes, and having him wash in the pool of Siloam?

Quiz 141

Plotting Against Jesus

*These questions are about the final days of Jesus' life
when the plot to kill Him reached a fever pitch.
How much do you remember about these events?*

1. Fill in the blank: Because Jesus ate with sinners and publicans, Jesus quoted His critics as saying, "Behold a man gluttonous, and a _____."

2. Why did the Pharisees watch to see if Jesus would heal the man with the withered hand on the Sabbath day?
    a) The man was well-beloved by the Jewish people.
    b) They believed Jesus could not do the miracle.
    c) They sought a reason to accuse Him.
    d) They wished to see a miracle.

3. True or False: After Jesus healed the woman who was bent double on the Sabbath day, the ruler of the synagogue accused Jesus of working on the Sabbath day.

4. Fill in the blank: The Jews sought to kill Jesus because He said that "God was his Father, making himself _____ with God."

5. Fill in the blank: "Then went the Pharisees, and took counsel how they might _____ him in his talk."

6. True or False: After Jesus answered questions by the Pharisees, Sadducees, and a lawyer, they sought all the more to trick Him with questions.

225

7. When the Herodians at the instigation of the Pharisees asked "Is it lawful to give tribute to Caesar," how did Jesus begin His answer?
   - a) "What think ye of Christ? whose son is he?"
   - b) "Why tempt ye me, ye hypocrites?"
   - c) "Ye do err, not knowing the scriptures, nor the power of God."
   - d) He did not answer because they had taken counsel to destroy him.

8. Although Jesus taught in the temple during the daytime, why were the chief priests and scribes careful in how they arrested Him?

9. What was the first question that Judas asked the chief priests?
   - a) "What shall be the sign of your coming?"
   - b) "What sign shall I give you that it is time to betray him?"
   - c) "What will ye give me, and I will deliver him unto you?"
   - d) "Whatever that thou doest, can thou do it quickly?"

10. Choose A or B: The chief priests and other officials were A) glad B) reluctant to use Judas Iscariot to betray Jesus.

Quiz 142

The Last Supper

Jesus ate a final meal with His disciples on the night
He was betrayed. What happened at this "last supper"?

1. Which two disciples did Jesus send to prepare the
   Passover meal?
   > a) Matthew and Simon Zelotes   c) Peter and John
   > b) James and Andrew   d) Thomas and
   >   Judas Iscariot

2. When the disciples were looking for a guest chamber
   where Jesus and His disciples could eat the Passover, they
   met a man carrying what?

3. What did Simon Peter first say when Jesus said He would
   wash Peter's feet?
   > a) "Am I the one who is not clean?"
   > b) "Lord, not my feet only, but those of the others, as well."
   > c) "The servant is not greater than his lord."
   > d) "Thou shalt never wash my feet."

4. Why did Jesus wash the feet of His disciples?

5. True or False: When Jesus said the betrayer was among
   the twelve apostles, Simon Peter asked Jesus directly,
   "Lord, who is it?"

6. Fill in the blank: In speaking of the bread at the Last Supper, Jesus said, "This is my _____ which is given for you: this do in remembrance of me."

7. What does Jesus say the fruit of the vine represents?

8. How many times did Jesus say Peter would deny Him before the cock crowed?

9. Fill in the blank: Peter said, "Lord, I am ready to go with thee, both into _____, and to death."

10. Before going out into the Mount of Olives, what did Jesus and the disciples do?
    a) gathered the uneaten food
    b) paid the rent on the upper room
    c) prayed
    d) sang a hymn

Quiz 143

Jesus' Arrest

Who arrested Jesus, and how did it happen?
These questions test your recall of that night in the
garden when His enemies closed in on Him.

1. True or False: When the cock crowed the third time, Jesus was blindfolded.

2. Jesus told His apostles it was written that He would be reckoned among whom?
  a) the firstborn   c) the Levites
  b) the leaders of nations   d) the transgressors

3. What was the name of the garden where Jesus prayed?

4. Choose A or B: When Jesus prayed in the garden, He asked that the hour might A) pass from Him B) come quickly.

5. Fill in the blank: "The spirit indeed is willing, but the flesh is _____."

6. How many times did Jesus pray the same words?

7. What did Jesus tell those who came to arrest Him at night?
  a) "Nothing is secret that shall not be made manifest."
  b) "The children of this world are wiser than the children of light."
  c) "This is your hour, and the power of darkness."
  d) "You keep your wrath in secret until the appointed time."

8. When Jesus stated that He was the one they sought, what happened to the band of men who came to arrest Him?
  a) They heard the voices of angels.
  b) They rushed forward and bound Jesus.
  c) They went backward, and fell to the ground.
  d) They were momentarily struck blind by a great light.

9. Which ear of Malchus did Peter cut off with the sword?

10. Fill in the blanks: Jesus told Peter, "Put up again thy _____ into his place: for all they that take the _____ shall perish with the _____."

Quiz 144

A Traitor's End

Most of us know that Jesus was betrayed by Judas, one of His disciples. What else do you know about this disciple-turned-traitor?

1. True or False: When Jesus announced at the Last Supper that He would be betrayed by one of the Twelve, most of the apostles suspected Judas.

2. How did Judas identify Jesus to the multitude that came to arrest Him?

3. How many pieces of silver did the chief priests and elders pay Judas to betray Jesus?

4. Fill in the blank: Judas said, "I have sinned in that I have betrayed the innocent _____."

5. Why did the priests use the betrayer's money to buy a field rather than put it in the treasury?

6. How did Judas kill himself?
    a) cast himself down from a high place
    b) fell on his sword
    c) hanged himself
    d) hung a millstone from his neck and drowned in the sea

7. The chief priests bought the potter's field to use for what purpose?

8. In addition to Aceldama, the potter's field was also known by what other name?

9. According to Peter, the apostle who replaced Judas must have been a witness of what?
    a) a miracle of Jesus
    b) His resurrection
    c) His preaching
    d) John the Baptist's preaching about Jesus

10. Who replaced Judas and was numbered with the other apostles?
    a) Barsabas
    b) Joseph
    c) Justus
    d) Matthias

Jesus' Trial

After appearing before the Jewish Sanhedrin, Jesus was placed on trial before the Roman governor, Pontius Pilate. Review this event by answering the questions in this quiz.

1. Why did the chief priests and elders who brought Jesus to Pontius Pilate's judgment hall not enter it themselves?

2. What was one of the charges that the crowd brought against Jesus when He was before Pilate?
    a) He brought Gentiles into the temple.
    b) He claimed a kingdom not of this world.
    c) He claimed He would destroy the temple in forty days.
    d) He objected to giving tribute to Caesar.

3. What did the chief priests say when Pilate told them to judge Jesus according to their law?

4. What three-word question did Pilate ask when Jesus said, "To this end was I born. . .that I should bear witness unto the truth"?

5. True or False: Pilate sent Jesus to Herod because Jesus was from Judaea.

6. Fill in the blank: When Pilate asked if he should crucify their king, the chief priests said, "We have no king but _____."

7. Whose wife said she had suffered many things in a dream because of Jesus?

    a) the wife of Caiaphas   c) the wife of Pilate

    b) the wife of Herod   d) the wife of the chief of
                                        the Praetorium guard

8. When the soldiers mocked Jesus, what did they put in His right hand?

9. What did the guards say when they mocked Jesus and saluted Him?

    a) "Behold the man!"

    b) "Bow down and worship us!"

    c) "Hail, King of the Jews!"

    d) "Tell us the color of your robe!"

10. What did Herod hope to see Jesus do?

Quiz 146

The Crucifixion

*Jesus died for our sins when He was executed on a cross.
These questions should make you thankful
for the sacrifice He made for us.*

1. Who was the person compelled to bear the cross of Jesus?

2. What is the meaning of "Golgotha," the place where Jesus was crucified?

3. At His crucifixion, what were the first words that Jesus said?

  a) "Father, forgive them; for they know not what they do."
        a) "Father, forgive them; for they know not what they do."
        b) "I must be about my Father's business."
        c) "It is finished."
        d) He groaned with words that could not be understood.

4. Into how many pieces did the soldiers divide Jesus' garments?

5. What was the inscription placed above Jesus?

6. True or False: Although Jesus is often shown between two thieves at the crucifixion, the Bible does not specify that Jesus was crucified in the middle.

7. What is the interpretation of the words "Eli, Eli, lama sabachthani" that Jesus uttered?

8. In His statement to His disciple, "Behold thy mother!" Jesus was speaking about which Mary?
        a) Mary Magdalene
        b) Mary, His mother
        c) Mary, the mother of John
        d) Mary, the wife of Cleophas

9. What happened starting at the sixth hour?
    a) Darkness was over all the land for three hours.
    b) The light of the sun became sevenfold.
    c) The shadows retreated ten degrees.
    d) The sun stood still.

10. When Jesus said, "I thirst," what was He offered?

Quiz 147

Jesus' Death

The death of Jesus was both tragic and triumphant—tragic because sin nailed Him to the cross but triumphant because He provided for our salvation through His death. How much do you remember about this pivotal event in world history?

1. Fill in the blanks: Although one man ran for vinegar, the others said, "Let be, let us see whether Elias (Elijah) will come to _____ him."

2. What method was used to raise vinegar to Jesus' lips?
    a) a cup raised by the centurion
    b) a sponge raised on a hyssop reed
    c) a linen cloth soaked in vinegar
    d) none; the soldiers forbade giving Him vinegar

3. Following the death of Jesus, what happened at the temple?
    a) No stone was left upon another.
    b) The cherubims fell face down.
    c) The Pharisees gnashed their teeth and tore their clothes.
    d) The veil of the temple was torn from top to bottom.

4. True or False: Tombs were opened and saints came forth and marched to Golgotha as witnesses of Jesus' holiness.

5. Fill in the blank: The centurion said, "_____ this was the Son of God."

6. The centurion's statement about Jesus being the Son of God was made shortly after what event?
    a) the earthquake
    b) when he pierced Jesus' side
    c) when Jesus was found to be dead
    d) when they came for the body of Jesus

7. True or False: Some of the women who viewed the crucifixion from afar had followed Jesus from Galilee and ministered to Him.

8. Why did the Jews want the bodies taken down from the crosses before sunset?

9. What method was used to ensure the two men crucified with Jesus were dead?

10. Fill in the blank: "They shall look on him whom they _____."

Quiz 148

The Burial of Jesus

How and where was the body of Jesus buried?
Test your recall by answering the questions in this quiz.

1. The women looking on from afar included Mary the mother of Joses and what other Mary?

2. Who asked Pilate for the body of Jesus?
    a) Joseph of Arimathaea
    b) Nicodemus
    c) Simon of Cyrene
    d) the sons of Zebedee

3. Who did Pilate question to ensure that Jesus was dead?

4. True or False: The person who brought a mixture of myrrh and aloes to prepare Jesus' body is not named in the Bible.

5. In addition to the spices, how was the body of Jesus wrapped?
    a) in a coat of many colors
    b) in a garment without seam
    c) in a clean linen cloth
    d) in a purple robe

6. Fill in the blank: The Pharisees told Pilate, "Sir, we remember that that _____ said. . .After three days I will rise again."

7. Who had been buried in the tomb where Jesus was laid?
   a) Joseph of Arimathaea's father
   b) Lazarus
   c) the owner of the garden
   d) no one

8. How had the tomb been constructed?

9. How was the tomb sealed?

10. True or False: Pilate sent soldiers to seal the tomb and
    set a watch.

Quiz 149

He Is Risen!

*The forces of evil and death were defeated when
Jesus arose from the grave. How much about
His resurrection do you remember?*

1. Who rolled the stone away from the grave?
   a) a gardener dressed in white   c) the guards
   b) an angel   d) the women

2. What day of the week was it when the women found the
   tomb empty?

3. Fill in the blank: "Why seek ye the living among the _____?"

4. When Peter and the "other disciple" ran to the tomb, which one arrived first?

5. What part of Jesus' burial cloths was rolled separate from the others?

6. To whom did Jesus appear first?

7. When the chief priests and elders learned about the empty tomb, what did they do to the soldiers who were guarding it?
   - a) sent them to a far country
   - b) shut them in prison
   - c) beat them and commanded them not to speak about the matter
   - d) gave them money

8. How many disciples were on the road to Emmaus when Jesus appeared to them?

9. True or False: The disciples on the road to Emmaus instantly recognized Jesus.

10. The disciples on the road to Emmaus invited Jesus to do what with them?
    - a) return to Jerusalem to learn more about the events of the day
    - b) spend the night with them
    - c) stop at a well while they went and bought meat
    - d) read Esaias the prophet with them

Quiz 150

More on the Resurrection

These questions focus on Jesus' appearances to His followers after His resurrection. What did He say and do in these post-resurrection appearances?

1. On the evening of the day of Jesus' resurrection, why had the disciples shut the doors of the room where they met?
    a) because of the press of the people
    b) because of their confusion
    c) for fear of the Jews
    d) to keep out Jesus' followers who fled at His arrest

2. What were the first words that Jesus said to His disciples in the room?

3. What effect did Jesus' appearance have upon His disciples?
    a) They fell back as if dead.
    b) They rejoiced with exceedingly great joy.
    c) They said, "Forgive us our unbelief."
    d) They were terrified.

4. What did Jesus eat when He met with the disciples in the room?

5. Fill in the blank: "Repentance and _____ of sins should be preached in his name among all nations."

6. Why did Jesus tell His disciples to wait in the city?
   a) so persecution would not take root
   b) to be filled with power from the Holy Spirit
   c) to ordain another to replace Judas
   d) to wait for Him to be taken from them

7. True or False: At His first appearance to the disciples, Jesus did not show them His hands or His side.

8. Who was not present when Jesus first appeared to the disciples in the room?

9. Jesus once again appeared in the locked room after how many days?

10. Fill in the blank: "Blessed are they that have not _____, and yet have believed."

Quiz 151

The Ascension

Jesus ascended back to His father after spending some time with His disciples. What happened during these days leading up to His ascension?

1. Fill in the blanks: Jesus told His disciples, "For John truly baptized with water; but ye shall be baptized with the _____ _____."

2. How many times did Jesus ask Peter, "Lovest thou me"?

3. True or False: The "disciple whom Jesus loved" was told that he would not see death.

4. Fill in the blank: Jesus said, "All _____ is given unto me in heaven and in earth."

5. What five-word phrase is missing from this quotation of the Great Commission: "Go ye therefore, and teach all nations, baptizing them in the name of the Father, and of the Son, and of the Holy Ghost: Teaching them to observe all things: and, lo, I am with you always, even unto the end of the world."

6. Where did Jesus lead His disciples when He blessed them and was carried up into heaven?
     a) Bethany   c) Jerusalem
     b) Galilee   d) the Upper Room

7. How many days elapsed between the time of Jesus' resurrection and His ascension?

8. When Jesus showed Himself at the Sea of Tiberias, how many fish did Peter catch when Jesus told him to cast the net on the right side of the boat?
     a) 2   c) a multitude that broke the net
     b) 153   d) none

9. How was Jesus received out of the disciples' sight?
     a) in a cloud   c) in a flaming chariot
     b) in a whirlwind   d) He vanished from sight

10. Where did the disciples go after Jesus left them?

Quiz 152

Pentecost

*The Pentecost experience energized the disciples
and transformed them into bold witnesses. How many
questions about this great event can you answer?*

1. On the day of Pentecost, how does the writer of Acts
   describe the sound from heaven?

2. In addition to hearing in their own languages, what else
   about the speakers caused the multitude to be amazed?
   a) They asked not permission to speak.
   b) They performed miracles as a sign of faith.
   c) They were Galilaeans.
   d) They were the sons of local merchants.

3. What did the mockers say about those who spoke in
   tongues?

4. Who was the prophet who said, "Your sons and your
   daughters shall prophesy"?

5. What would the old men do in the last days?
   a) dream dreams
   b) rise up at the voice of a bird
   c) see visions
   d) see wonders in heaven

6. Fill in the blank: "Jesus of Nazareth. . .ye have taken, and by _____ hands have crucified and slain."

7. Fill in the blank: At the end of Peter's sermon, the listeners were "_____ in their heart[s]."

8. True or False: To those who asked what they should do, Peter said, "Tarry in Jerusalem and it shall be told unto you."

9. How many souls were added to the church on Pentecost?

10. Who "added to the church daily such as should be saved"?
    a) believers   c) the Holy Spirit
    b) Peter   d) the Lord

Quiz 153

The Church Grows

Church growth is not a new idea; the early church grew rapidly as people accepted Jesus as Savior. This quiz reviews how this growth occurred.

1. Fill in the blank: "And they continued stedfastly in the apostles' doctrine and fellowship, and in breaking of bread, and in _____."

2. True or False: Philip found the people cold to his message, shook the dust from his feet, and went to Gaza.

3. Fill in the blank: After Peter's address at the temple following the healing of the lame man, the number of men who believed was about _____ thousand.

4. What is the meaning of the name Barnabas?

5. What did Barnabas sell so he could put the money at the apostles' feet?
    a) a pearl of great price   c) land
    b) "a possession"   d) livestock

6. The people came to what location as the apostles performed signs and wonders?
    a) the Beautiful gate   c) Solomon's porch
    b) the sheep market   d) the temple stairs

7. After the death of Stephen and the persecution of the church, to what city did Philip travel first?
    a) Decapolis   c) Judea
    b) Galilee   d) Samaria

8. To provide for those who had need, what did the believers do?

9. What was the first question that Philip asked the eunuch of Ethiopia?

10. How does the Scripture that the eunuch of Ethiopia was reading begin?
    a) "He will swallow up death in victory."
    b) "Prepare ye the way of the Lord."

c) "He was led as a sheep to the slaughter."

d) "The stone which the builders refused is become the head stone."

Martyrdom

Stephen was the first martyr of the Christian movement. How much do you remember about his ministry and his death?

1. As the number of disciples multiplied, murmuring began between what two groups of Christians?

2. Fill in the blank: The twelve apostles said it was not good for them to leave preaching and instead serve _____.

3. How is Stephen described?
   a) "a man devoid of hypocrisy and iniquity"
   b) "a man full of faith and of the Holy Ghost"
   c) "a man of sorrows"
   d) "a proselyte of Antioch"

4. True or False: Unlike the apostles, Stephen performed no miracles.

5. What charge did the false accusers bring against Stephen?
   a) He possessed books of sorcery.
   b) He spoke blasphemous words against Moses.
   c) He swore against the authorities in high places.
   d) He was a false prophet and a false teacher.

6. Fill in the blank: "Which of the prophets have not your fathers _____ ?"

7. True or False: When Stephen recounted the story of Israel from Abraham to Solomon and the prophets, the Jewish leaders were cut to the heart.

8. What statement did Stephen make that resulted in the Jewish leaders rushing upon him to kill him?
   a) "I see. . .the Son of man standing on the right hand of God."
   b) "Jesus shall change the customs which Moses delivered us."
   c) "The Most High dwelleth not in temples made with hands."
   d) "Who made you my ruler and judge?"

9. What role did Saul have in the stoning of Stephen?

10. What were Stephen's final words?

Quiz 155

Persecution of Christians

Persecution actually caused the early church to grow as believers fled, sharing their faith with others wherever they went. This quiz should impress you with the faith of these early Christians.

1. Who does Peter say gathered against the holy child Jesus?
   a) Herod and Pontus Pilate   c) the Gentiles
   b) the people of Israel   d) all of the above

2. After the apostles were put in a common prison, where did the angel of the Lord who opened the doors tell them to go and speak?
   a) by the seaside
   b) at the marketplace
   c) at the temple
   d) to leave Jerusalem and go to Galilee

3. Fill in the blanks: When told to keep silent about Jesus, Peter and the other apostles answered, "We ought to obey _____ rather than _____."

4. True or False: Gamaliel is the person who said, "If it be of God, ye cannot overthrow it."

5. Which apostle did Herod kill?

6. Which apostle did Herod put in prison?

7. Who was the person who persecuted the church and put both men and women in prison?

8. After Paul's conversion, when his enemies were laying in wait for him by the gates of the city of Damascus, how did Paul escape?

9. What action did Gamaliel propose to the council in dealing with the apostles?
    a) beat and release them
    b) place them under house arrest
    c) let them alone
    d) tell them not to speak about Jesus

10. Although persecution of the church in Jerusalem scattered the believers after the death of Stephen, who remained in Jerusalem?

Quiz 156

Conversion of Saul

Saul's conversion transformed him from a persecutor of the church into a proclaimer of the gospel. How much do you remember about his dramatic turnaround?

1. Fill in the blank: "Saul, yet breathing out threatenings and _____ against the disciples of the Lord. . ."

2. Paul traveled to Damascus to take believers bound to what place?

    a) Antioch   c) Rome

    b) Jerusalem   d) the synagogue at Damascus

3. When Jesus said, "Saul, Saul, why persecutest thou me?" what was the first question that Paul asked?

4. True or False: Jesus told Saul what he must do and sent Ananias to comfort him.

5. How many days was Paul without sight?

6. When the Lord spoke to Ananias, how did Ananias reply?

    a) "Can any good thing come out of Tarsus?"

    b) "Much evil he hath done to thy saints at Jerusalem."

    c) "He hath made himself vile at the stoning of Stephen."

    d) "Speak, Lord; for thy servant heareth. Here am I, send me."

7. In addition to kings and the children of Israel, to whom else would Saul bear the name of Jesus?

8. Fill in the blank: When Ananias entered the house where Paul was staying and put his hand on Saul, Ananias said, "_____ Saul, the Lord, even Jesus. . .hath sent me."

9. After being strengthened and spending time with the disciples at Damascus, what did Saul do?

    a) preached Christ in the synagogues in Damascus

    b) returned to Jerusalem to meet with the apostles

c) visited those he had put in prison

d) went to Arabia

10. After Saul's conversion, what did the Jews take counsel to do?

Quiz 157

Peter the Leader

*The apostle Peter was one of the strongest leaders
in the early church. How many of these questions
about his contribution can you answer?*

1. After healing the lame man, Peter told the crowd at the temple that they had denied Christ in the presence of A) Pilate B) Caesar.

2. At the temple, who did Peter say fulfilled the promise that the world would be blessed through Abraham?

3. When Peter was asked by what name or authority he healed the lame man, how did he answer?
    a) "by the name of Jesus Christ of Nazareth"
    b) "Having eyes, see ye not? and having ears, hear ye not?"
    c) "The lame man is of age; ask him."
    d) Peter did not answer.

4. Cornelius was a centurion of which band?

5. How does Acts describe the religious nature of Cornelius?
   a) "A devout man, and one that. . .prayed to God"
   b) "A just man. . .who would not see death until he received salvation"
   c) "A seeker of truth. . .who searched for the Kingdom of God"
   d) "One sanctified by the Holy Spirit"

6. True or False: After the vision from God, Cornelius traveled to Joppa to see Peter.

7. After seeing the vision of unclean animals let down as in a sheet, what did the Lord tell Peter to do?

8. Fill in the blanks: Peter said, "Not so, Lord; for I have never eaten any thing that is _____ or _____."

9. Who said, "God is no respecter of persons"?
   a) Cornelius
   b) Peter
   c) the angel who spoke to Cornelius during his vision
   d) the angel who spoke to Peter during his vision

10. What did Peter command Cornelius and his household to do?

Quiz 158

Miracles of the Apostles

*Many miracles performed by the apostles are recorded
in the book of Acts. This quiz should impress
you with their power and authority.*

1. When Peter and John saw the lame man at the gate of the
   temple, who said, "Silver and gold have I none"?
   a) John
   b) Peter
   c) the lame man
   d) the lame man's mother

2. Besides walking and leaping, what else did the lame man
   do when he went with Peter and John into the temple?

3. True or False: The high priests and other Jewish leaders
   denied that Peter and John had healed the lame man.

4. The lame man had been lame for how long?

5. Who did Peter heal at Lydda?
   a) Aeneas, who had palsy
   b) an unnamed beggar who was lame
   c) Elymas, who was blind
   d) Gazelle, who had an issue of blood

6. What miracle involving Tabitha, also known as Dorcas,
   did Peter perform at Joppa?

7. What did the widows show Peter that Dorcas had made?

8. How did Paul say that Elymas, also known as Bar-jesus, would be punished?

9. Choose A or B: The people of Lystra and Derbe of Lycaonia said, "The gods are come down to us in the likeness of men" because Paul had A) healed a lame man B) brought fire down from heaven.

10. Who was preaching when the young man Eutychus went to sleep and fell to his death from the third loft?

Quiz 159

Paul's First Missionary Journey

Where did Paul travel, and what did he do during his first missionary journey? Find out by answering these questions.

1. What was the name of the deputy in Salamis on the island of Cyprus whom Barnabas and Saul ministered to, who had a name similar to Paul's Gentile name?

2. Who left Paul and Barnabas and returned to Jerusalem?

3. At Antioch in Pisida, what did the rulers of the synagogue say to Paul and his company?
   a) "Speak not evil of the rulers of our people."
   b) "If ye have any word of exhortation for the people, say on."
   c) "Only the just shall sit and teach."
   d) "Yet are full of subtlety. . .and all mischief."

4. Choose A or B: Paul quotes the statement, "Thou art my Son, this day have I begotten thee" from A) the preaching of John the Baptist B) the second Psalm.

5. Fill in the blanks: "And by him all that believe are _____ from all things, from which ye could not be _____ by the law of Moses."

6. Why was Paul called Mercurius in Lystra?
   a) He could think quickly on his feet.
   b) He drove a chariot furiously.
   c) He was the chief speaker.
   d) Mercurius was the chief god of the city.

7. Why did the priest of Jupiter at Lystra bring oxen and garlands to the gates?
   a) to counter the preaching of Paul
   b) to give as tribute to the Jewish synagogue
   c) to sacrifice to Paul and Barnabas as gods
   d) to show the superior power of his god

8. Fill in the blank: "[God] in times past _____ all nations to walk in their own ways."

9. What did Paul and Barnabas ordain in every church?

10. When Paul and Barnabas returned to Antioch, they told all that God had done through them and how God had opened the door of faith to what people?

Quiz 160

The Jerusalem Council

Leaders of the early church gathered in Jerusalem to deal with a controversial issue. This quiz identifies the issue and tells how they dealt with it.

1. The believing Pharisees in Jerusalem said that Gentile believers must be circumcised and do what else?

2. Who said, "God made choice. . .that the Gentiles by my mouth should hear the word of the gospel"?

3. Fill in the blank: "God. . .put no _____ between us and them, purifying their hearts by faith."

4. What did Barnabas and Saul declare to the Jerusalem council?
   a) "Faith only shall save them."
   b) "The law of Moses was a yoke we were not able to bear."

    c) "Trouble not them, which among the Gentiles are
      turned to God."

    d) They declared the miracles and wonders that God
      had done among the Gentiles.

5. Who was the last speaker at the council who listed the things Gentile believers should do?

6. In addition to Paul and Barnabas, who else accompanied messengers from the council to Antioch?
    a) John Mark and Peter
    b) Judas and Silas
    c) Luke and James
    d) Timothy and Matthew

7. True or False: The letter to the Gentiles specifically stated that the apostle's previous command to keep the law of Moses had been in error.

8. What term in the letter is used to describe Paul and Barnabas?
    a) apostles born out of due season
    b) friends of faith
    c) men who "hazarded their lives" for the name of Jesus
    d) ministers to the Gentiles

9. The letter from the council lists how many things to avoid?

10. Choose A or B: After hearing the things forbidden to them, the people in Antioch A) lamented B) rejoiced.

Paul's Second Missionary Journey

The apostle Paul always seemed to be going into a different territory to tell people about Jesus. This quiz reviews what happened on his second missionary journey.

1. Fill in the blank: The keeper of the prison "took them the same hour of the night, and washed their stripes; and was _____, he and all his, straightway."

2. Who prevented Paul and his company from going into Asia to preach the Word?
   a) the Holy Ghost
   b) Roman authorities
   c) rulers of the synagogues
   d) those who cared about Paul's safety

3. The man Paul saw in the vision who said, "Come. . .help us" was from what region?
   a) Italy   c) Spain
   b) Macedonia   d) Syria

4. Choose A or B: The masters of the young woman in Philippi A) rejoiced B) were upset when Paul cast from her the spirit of divination.

5. What did Lydia sell?

6. Who was the son of a Jewish mother and Gentile father who joined Paul's company at Lystra?

7. The Jews of which synagogue are described as "more noble"?
    a) Berea   c) Lystra
    b) Derbe   d) Thessalonica

8. What was written on the altar that Paul mentions to the philosophers at Athens?

9. Fill in the blank: "For in him we live, and move, and have our _____."

10. What were the names of the husband and wife tent-makers who Paul stayed with in Corinth?

Quiz 162

Paul's Third Missionary Journey

Paul is off again—this time on mission trip number three. See how much you remember about this famous journey.

1. True or False: Apollos was described as an eloquent man but unlearned in the Scriptures.

2. Fill in the blanks: In Ephesus, Paul found believers who had not heard of the _____ _____.

3. Fill in the blank: When the vagabond Jews tried to cast out an evil spirit, the evil spirit said, "Jesus I know, and _____ I know; but who are ye?"

4. What was the occupation of Demetrius, who stirred up opposition to Paul?
   - a) slave
   - b) gladiator
   - c) silversmith
   - d) weaver of fine linen prayer cloths

5. Where was the temple of Diana?
   - a) Ephesus
   - b) Laodicea
   - c) Sardis
   - d) Smyrna

6. Choose A or B: After the near riot by those who worshipped the goddess Diana, the town clerk told the people to A) beat Paul and put him in prison B) do nothing rashly.

7. Paul warned the believers at Ephesus to watch because what type of "grievous" animal would threaten the flock?

8. When speaking to the elders at Ephesus, who did Paul say had provided his necessities?
   - a) believers at Jerusalem
   - b) elders at Ephesus
   - c) Lydia and other wealthy women
   - d) Paul's own hands

9. Who said, "It is more blessed to give than to receive"?

10. Why were the believers at Ephesus sorrowful as Paul left them for Jerusalem?

Quiz 163

Apostle on Trial

Paul was falsely accused by Jewish leaders in Jerusalem and held as a prisoner by Roman officials in Caesarea. How did he conduct himself during this time?

1. True or False: The believers in Jerusalem urged Paul to publicly reject the Jewish law.

2. Who did the Jews from Asia think Paul had brought into the temple?
    a) a Roman soldier
    b) an unbelieving Egyptian
    c) an unpurified Jew
    d) Greeks

3. Paul spoke from the castle stairs to the mob in what language?

4. Why did the chief captain, or Roman military officer, decide not to question Paul by scourging?

5. What was Festus's concern about sending Paul to Caesar?

6. Fill in the blank: Felix told Paul, "When I have a _____ season, I will call for thee."

7. Paul caused a dissension at the Jewish council over what issue?
    a) purification
    b) meat offered to idols
    c) paying tribute to Caesar
    d) the resurrection

8. True or False: Paul said that King Agrippa believed the prophets.

9. Fill in the blank: Agrippa said to Paul, "Almost thou _____ me to be a Christian."

10. King Agrippa told Festus that Paul might have been set free except for what reason?
    a) He convicted himself by his own lips by confessing past persecutions.
    b) If he had not appealed to Caesar.
    c) One man should die to ensure their rule.
    d) They needed to try him to please the Jewish leaders.

Quiz 164

Roman Non-Holiday

The book of Acts comes to a close with Paul's voyage to Rome and his witness for Christ while imprisoned in this city. This quiz should impress you with God's providential care for His "apostle to the Gentiles."

1. Choose A or B: The centurion Julius treated Paul
   A) courteously B) with distain.

2. Fill in the blank: Despite Paul's warning, the captain of the ship decided to sail on to winter in Phenice, a haven on the island of _____.

3. On the third day, what did the sailors toss overboard?
   a) the cargo of wheat
   b) the master and owner
   c) the false idols
   d) the tackling of the ship

4. What person did the angel tell Paul he must be brought before?

5. How many people did Paul say would die because of the shipwreck?

6. How did the people on the island treat the shipwrecked survivors?

7. When the people saw Paul bitten by the viper, what was their first thought?
   a) Paul could heal their sick.
   b) Paul was a god.
   c) Paul was a murderer.
   d) Paul was responsible for the shipwreck.

8. True or False: When Paul spoke to the Jews in Rome, they said that all Jews in the city were in an uproar over him.

9. Fill in the blank: "The salvation of God is sent unto the _____, and that they will hear it."

10. During the two years Paul was in Rome, how did he spend his time?
    a) in prison bound between two soldiers
    b) preaching while living in a hired house
    c) preaching while living in the home of Aquila and Priscilla
    d) working in a tent-making shop while awaiting trial

A Letter to Rome

*This quiz comes from the first five chapters of Paul's
letter to the Roman Christians. What themes
from these chapters can you identify?*

1. In addition to the promise of Holy Scriptures, what
   specific event declared that Jesus was the Son of God?
   a) His humble birth of a virgin
   b) His baptism by John
   c) His triumph over the tempter after fasting forty days
   d) His resurrection from the dead

2. Fill in the blank: "For I am not _____ of the gospel of
   Christ: for it is the power of God unto salvation."

3. Fill in the blank: "For there is no _____ of persons with God."

4. What phrase completes this quotation "There is none
   righteous. . ."?
   a) "except the Holy One."
   b) "no, not one."
   c) "not of men, but of God."
   d) "without circumcision of the heart."

5. In describing the unprofitable ones, what does Paul say
   that their feet are swift to do?

6. Paul says that all have sinned, and come short of what?

7. Which statement summarizes a conclusion by Paul in the letter to the Romans?
   a) A man is justified by faith.
   b) A man is justified by works of the law.
   c) God is love.
   d) Hypocrites shall not enter heaven.

8. True or False: Where no law is, sin has no remission.

9. What does tribulation "worketh"?

10. Paul writes that Christ died for us, while we were yet what?

Quiz 166

Dead or Alive

These questions cover chapters 6 through 8 of the book of Romans. What hope does Paul offer in these chapters to people who are spiritually dead because of their sin?

1. Fill in the blank: "What shall we say then? Shall we continue in sin, that _____ may abound?"

2. True or False: When baptized into Jesus Christ, believers are also baptized into His life.

3. What are the wages of sin?

4. How long does the law have dominion over a person?

5. What made believers dead to the law?

6. What aspect of Paul delights in the law of God?
   a) the carnal man
   b) the inward man
   c) the warring of his mind
   d) the wretched man

7. The Spirit bears witness with whose spirit that believers are the sons of God?
   a) the believer's spirit
   b) the Spirit of Jesus
   c) the spirit of the old man
   d) the spirit of those chosen to serve the children of Israel

8. Choose A or B: According to Paul, real hope is A) seen B) not seen.

9. Fill in the blank: "And we know that all things work together for _____ to them that love God."

10. What phrase completes the statement, "If God be for us. . ."?
    a) "then all enemies shall flee."
    b) "then all paths lead to righteousness."
    c) "who can be against us?"
    d) "why shall we suffer for the faith?"

Quiz 167

The Rest of Romans

Romans chapters 9–16 are the focus of this quiz.
How much do you recall about the themes of these chapters?

1. According to Paul, what does the potter have power over?

2. Paul says that faith comes in what way?
    a) by hearing
    b) by laying on of hands
    c) by prayer and fasting
    d) by seeing miracles

3. Paul was an Israelite of the seed of Abraham and of what tribe?

4. Fill in the blank: "O the depth of the _____ both of the wisdom and knowledge of God!"

5. Paul called on the Romans to present their bodies in what way?
    a) as a living sacrifice
    b) as pure as celestial bodies
    c) quickened by the Spirit
    d) to be burned

6. Paul says not to be overcome with evil, but overcome evil how?

7. True or False: Paul tells believers to obey rulers and pay tribute.

8. Fill in the blank: "Him that is weak in the faith receive ye, but not to _____ disputations."

9. Paul had plans to visit the believers in Rome and then go to what country?
   a) Egypt
   b) Gaul
   c) Spain
   d) the New World

10. Paul says to salute one another how?

Quiz 168

Letter to a Church in Trouble

Paul addressed sin and divisions in the church at Corinth in chapters 1–6 of 1 Corinthians. How much do you remember about his advice to these believers in these chapters?

1. Fill in the blank: "For other _____ can no man lay than that is laid, which is Jesus Christ."

2. How does Paul say that the Greeks view Christ crucified?
   a) a deceiver who entered the world
   b) a stumbling block
   c) a fulfillment of the law
   d) foolishness

3. To the Corinthians, Paul says he is determined not to know anything save Jesus and Him how?
   a) as a shepherd leading His flock
   b) crucified
   c) on the right hand of God
   d) with a righteous sword of truth

4. Because they were unable to bear meat, what did Paul feed the Corinthians?

5. Paul said that he planted, Apollos watered, but what had God done?
   a) captured the righteous
   b) given the increase
   c) purged the tares from the harvest
   d) released the bound sinner

6. After quoting the statements that the Corinthians made, "I am of Paul; and I am of Apollos," what question about division does Paul ask?

7. Choose A or B: Paul says that the wisdom of the world is A) foolishness B) craftiness with God.

8. Who did Paul send to the Corinthians that he described as "my beloved son"?

9. Fill in the blank: "Do ye not know that the saints shall judge the _____?"

10. Fill in the blanks: "What? know ye not that your body is the temple of the _____ _____?"

Quiz 169

Paul on Marriage

This quiz covers only one chapter in 1 Corinthians—chapter 7. What did Paul have to say about marriage in this chapter?

1. After saying it is good for a man not to touch a woman, in his "nevertheless" statement that follows, what does Paul say about every man?

2. After saying that the wife has not power of her own body, what does Paul say of the husband concerning his body?

3. Fill in the blank: "It is better to marry than to _____."

4. Fill in the blanks: "Let every man abide in the same _____ wherein he was _____."

5. Paul states that if a wife departs from her husband, she should either remain unmarried or do what?
    a) be reconciled only if her husband is a believer
    b) be reconciled to her husband
    c) remarry after being purified
    d) remarry only her husband's brother after her husband has died

6. What completes the statement "Art thou bound unto a wife?"
    a) "put her away if an unbeliever"
    b) "rejoice in the bride of thy youth"
    c) "seek not to be loosed"
    d) "ye shall have trouble in this age"

7. Choose A or B: He that is unmarried cares for the things that A) belong to the Lord B) are of the world.

8. A married woman cares for what?
    a) for her children above all else
    b) for the fashions of this world
    c) how she may please her husband
    d) the things of the Lord

9. Paul says that he who gives his virgin in marriage does well, but he who gives her not does what?

10. What phrase completes this statement: "But if her husband be dead, she is at liberty to be married to whom she will. . ."

Quiz 170

Spiritual Gifts

Paul's counsel on spiritual gifts in chapters 12–14 of 1 Corinthians is the focus of this quiz. These questions are a good summary of the Bible's major teachings on this subject.

1. Concerning spiritual gifts, Paul would not have the Corinthians what?
   a) carried away
   b) ignorant
   c) in sorrow
   d) slack concerning promises

2. Paul says that there are diversities of gifts, but the same what?

3. Fill in the blank: "But now are they many members, yet but one _____."

4. What would Paul be if he had the faith to remove mountains but had not charity?

5. Fill in the blanks: "When I was a _____, I spake as a _____, I understood as a _____, I thought as a _____."

6. True or False: Of faith, hope, and charity, only charity abides.

7. Choose A or B: Speaking in tongues with interpretation
   A) edifies the church B) confounds unbelievers.

8. Rather than speaking ten thousand words in an unknown tongue, Paul had rather speak how many words with understanding in the church?
   a) five
   b) forty
   c) seven times seventy
   d) any number to understanding ears

9. Tongues are a sign to whom?

10. Paul says that God is not the author of what?
    a) confusion   c) peace for the heathen
    b) eternal life   d) prosperity

Quiz 171

Our Resurrection

This important section of 1 Corinthians—chapter 15—contains Paul's teachings about the resurrection of believers. How do your views on this subject compare with Paul's?

1. Paul says that Christ died for our sins and rose again on the third day in accordance with what?

2. Who does Paul say was the first apostle to see the risen Christ?

3. True or False: Paul says that he regrets having never seen the risen Christ.

4. Fill in the blanks: "And if Christ be not risen, then is our preaching _____, and your faith is also _____."

5. How does Paul describe those in this life who have hope in Christ but not in the resurrection?
    a) The resurrection is for the just alone.
    b) We are of all men most miserable.
    c) We are sin-free regardless of future hope.
    d) We look to God who is God of the dead.

6. What is the last enemy that shall be destroyed?
    a) death   c) the evil one
    b) hell   d) unbelievers

7. Fill in the blanks: "Be not deceived: evil communications corrupt _____ _____."

8. After men, beasts, and fishes, what is the fourth type of flesh that Paul mentions?

9. In speaking of the resurrection in chapter 15, what does Paul say cannot inherit the kingdom of God?
    a) flesh and blood
    b) only those more righteous than the scribes and Pharisees
    c) only those with the fruit of the Spirit
    d) those who persecute the righteous

10. Death is swallowed up in what?

Another Letter to Corinth

*Paul dealt with several issues in his second
letter to the Corinthians. See how many
of them you can identify in this quiz.*

1. True or False: Paul wrote the believers at Corinth with much affliction and anguish of heart so that through his tears they would be grieved.

2. Who does Paul write one of his letters to and mention several times in this letter, describing him as "my brother" and "my partner and fellow helper"?
   a) John Mark   c) Barnabas
   b) Silas   d) Titus

3. Paul said he was made what kind of minister?
   a) a minister of the glory of the old law
   b) a minister of the letter of the new testament
   c) a minister of the spirit of the new testament
   d) a minister who destroys false teachers

4. When does Paul say the veil of Moses and the veil on the hearts of the children of Israel will be done away?

5. Choose A or B: The things that are seen are A) eternal B) temporal.

6. What does godly sorrow worketh?

7. After asking, "What agreement hath the temple of God with idols?" Paul says that believers are what?
   a) impure and defiled creatures
   b) light living in darkness
   c) the temple of God
   d) unequally yoked with idol worshippers

8. Fill in the blanks: "He which soweth _____ shall reap also _____; and he which soweth _____ shall reap also _____."

9. What kind of giver does God love?

10. Fill in the blank: "In the mouth of two or three _____ shall every word be established."

Quiz 173

Paul Defends Himself

This quiz is based on chapters 10–12 of 2 Corinthians. How many of these questions can you answer?

1. Fill in the blanks: "For though we walk in the _____, we do not war after the _____."

2. True or False: Paul says the weapons of the believer's warfare are carnal.

3. True or False: The children should lay up for the parents.

4. From the Jews, how many times did Paul receive forty stripes save one.

5. How many times did Paul suffer shipwreck?

6. For how long was Paul in the deep?

7. So that he would not be exalted above measure, Paul said he was given what?

8. What makes God's strength perfect?
   a) believers with the power to press on for the goal
   b) perfect obedience
   c) those who listen and obey Paul
   d) weakness

9. When Paul comes to Corinth for the third time, he tells them that he will be how?
   a) as a parent of unruly children
   b) not burdensome
   c) ready to stand against false prophets
   d) as keeper of the faith

10. Paul feared the minds of the Corinthian believers might be corrupted from what?
    a) the clarity of Paul's speech
    b) the offense of a crucified Christ
    c) by riches and cares of this world
    d) the simplicity that is in Christ

Quiz 174

Corinthians Fill-in-the-Blanks

*Fill-in-the-blanks questions are always a challenge.
See how many of these missing words you can identify
from your knowledge of 2 Corinthians.*

1. "Lest Satan should get an advantage of us: for we are not ignorant of his _____."

2. "Ye are our epistle written in our _____, known and read of all men."

3. "Now the Lord is that Spirit: and where the Spirit of the Lord is, there is _____."

4. "But we have this treasure in _____ vessels, that the excellency of the power may be of God, and not of us."
   a) glass   c) broken
   b) gold   d) earthen

5. "We are troubled on every side, yet not _____; we are perplexed, but not in _____."

6. "We have a building of God, an house not made with _____, eternal in the heavens."

7. "For we walk by _____, not by _____."

8. "Behold, now is the accepted _____; behold, now is the day of _____."

9. "Therefore if any man be in Christ, he is a new _____: old things are passed away; behold, all things are become new."

10. "For, when we were come into Macedonia, our flesh had no rest, but we were troubled on every side; without were _____, within were _____."
   a) fightings, fears
   c) restraints, animals
   b) frustrations, enemies
   d) bonds, conflicts

Quiz 175

Letter to the Galatians

Paul had some particularly strong words for the believers of Galatia. This quiz should impress you with his defense of the authentic gospel.

1. Who appointed Paul an apostle?
   a) Ananias and Barnabas
   b) Jesus Christ and God the Father
   c) the believers in Galatians
   d) the twelve apostles in Jerusalem

2. Concerning preaching the word of God, who does Paul say should be accursed?

3. What shall the just live by?

4. Choose A or B: A Christian is justified by A) the works of the law B) by the faith of Jesus Christ.

5. Paul says that those of the faith are the children of who?
     a) Abraham   c) Moses
     b) Adam   d) Noah

6. True or False: After becoming a Christian Paul immediately traveled to Jerusalem for instruction by the other apostles.

7. What does Paul say the law was?
     a) an embarrassing work of the flesh
     b) a schoolmaster
     c) a tender herb
     d) the old way cut down out of time

8. What does Paul say the Galatians would have plucked out and given to him?

9. Abraham's son born of promise was from the
     A) bondmaid B) freewoman.

10. In contrasting works of the flesh and fruit of the spirit, of which one does Paul say, "against such there is no law"?

Galatians Fill-in-the-Blanks

How well do you know Paul's letters to the Galatians?
These fill-in-the-blank questions should
be a real test of your knowledge.

1. "Our Lord Jesus Christ, who gave himself for our sins, that he might deliver us from this present _____ world. . ."
   a) materialistic   c) evil
   b) carnal   d) hopeless

2. "I am crucified with _____: nevertheless I live; yet not I, but _____ liveth in me."

3. "In thee [Abraham] shall all nations be _____."

4. "Christ hath redeemed us from the _____ of the law, being made a _____ for us."

5. "For as many of you as have been baptized into _____ have put on _____."

6. "For, brethren, ye have been called unto _____; only use not _____ for an occasion to the flesh, but by love serve one another."

7. "This I say then, Walk in the Spirit, and ye shall not fulfil the _____ of the flesh."

8. "If we live in the _____, let us also walk in the _____."

9. "Bear ye one another's _____, and so fulfil the law of Christ."
   a) garments   c) sins
   b) burdens   d) sickness

10. "Be not deceived; God is not mocked: for whatsoever a man soweth, that shall he also _____. For he that soweth to his flesh shall of the flesh _____ corruption; but he that soweth to the Spirit shall of the Spirit _____ life everlasting."

Quiz 177

Hello, Ephesus

This quiz focuses on chapters 1–4 of Paul's letter to the believers at Ephesus. You're a real biblical whiz if you can answer all these questions correctly.

1. Fill in the blank: "In whom we have redemption through his _____, the forgiveness of sins, according to the riches of his grace."

2. What has been put under the feet of Jesus?
   a) all things   c) the church
   b) sin and the grave   d) the evil one

3. Although the Ephesian believers were dead in sins, God is rich in what?

4. Following the statement, "For by grace are ye saved through faith," what else does Paul write?
    a) "and that not of yourselves: it is the gift of God"
    b) "by the works of righteous men"
    c) "by escaping from the Evil One"
    d) "even by zeal without knowledge"

5. Choose A or B: The Ephesians were A) Jews B) Gentiles.

6. The middle wall of partition that Jesus broke down refers to what?
    a) separation of men from women in temple worship
    b) separation of Jews and Gentiles
    c) separation of the Old and New Testament
    d) separation of the veil of the temple

7. Fill in the blanks: "There is _____ body, and _____ Spirit, even as ye are called in _____ hope of your calling."

8. Fill in the blanks: "And he gave _____, apostles; and _____, prophets; and _____, evangelists; and _____, pastors and teachers."

9. By what part of the day does Paul state that a person's wrath should be ended?

10. A person should work with his hands so he may have to give to whom?

Quiz 178

Practical Christian Living

*Chapters 5 and 6 of Paul's Ephesian letter give guidelines
for practical Christian living. How well do you
measure up to the standards in these chapters?*

1. Fill in the blank: Because God is the light, believers should
have no fellowship with the unfruitful works of _____.

2. Why should a believer "redeem the time"?
    a) because the days are evil
    b) because the morning will have fair skies
    c) because time is on their side
    d) because time waits for no man

3. Rather than being drunk with wine, believers should be
filled with what?
    a) a full knowledge of the law
    b) the Spirit
    c) the works of an ambassador
    d) with principle and power

4. In Ephesians, Paul compares a husband to his wife and
Christ to what?

5. What is the first commandment with promise?

6. True or False: Because God is a master in heaven, there is
respect of persons with Him.

7. Believers should put on the whole armor of God to stand against the wiles of who?

8. Paul in Ephesians says that believers do *not* wrestle against what?
   - a) angels
   - b) flesh and blood
   - c) men mightier than them
   - d) rulers of darkness

9. In the whole armor of God, what serves as the breastplate?
   - a) faith
   - b) gospel of peace
   - c) righteousness
   - d) truth

10. Fill in the blank: "Take the helmet of salvation, and the sword of the _____."

Quiz 179

A Word to the Philippians

Philippians is known as Paul's "epistle of joy."
These questions should show you why this is a fitting name.

1. Whether Christ is preached in pretence or in truth, what is Paul's reaction?
   - a) he is ashamed
   - b) he is conflicted
   - c) he is sorrowful
   - d) he rejoices

2. Fill in the blank: "For me to live is Christ, and to die is _____."

3. Rather than strife or vainglory, how should a believer esteem others?

4. What form did Jesus take when He was in the likeness of men?

5. Fill in the blank: Paul describes himself as a Hebrew of the _____.

6. Touching on the law, Paul was what?
    a) a Pharisee
    b) a proselyte Jew
    c) a Sadducee
    d) a scribe

7. How does Paul describe the peace of God?
    a) fully revealed in the gospel of Jesus Christ
    b) as a light
    c) as a rock
    d) passeth all understanding

8. After listing whatsoever things that are true, honest, just, pure, lovely, and of good report, what does Paul tell the Philippians to do?

9. Paul says that whatsoever state he is in, he has learned to be what?

10. Fill in the blank: "I can do all things through Christ which _____ me."

Quiz 180

Dear Colossians

*The supremacy of Christ for believers and the church
is the theme of Paul's epistle to the Colossians.
How well do you recall what he said in this letter?*

1. From what power has the Father delivered believers?

2. Paul says that God is A) visible B) invisible.

3. Fill in the blank: "And he is the head of the body, the
   _____."

4. What is one way that the Colossian believers might be
   spoiled?
   a) by purification of the law of Moses
   b) by the rudiments of Christ
   c) through philosophy and vain deceit
   d) by being careful of prayer

5. Where did Paul say for believers to set their affection?

6. In what musical way does Paul tell believers to teach and
   admonish one another?

7. Fill in the blank: "Whatsoever ye do in word or _____,
   do all in the name of the Lord Jesus."

8. With what should graceful speech be seasoned?

9. What charge does Paul give fathers concerning their
children?
    a) Give thanks for them.
    b) Love them.
    c) Do not provoke them to anger.
    d) Teach them to walk in wisdom.

10. What phrase does Paul use to describe his friend Luke?
    a) beloved physician
    b) faithful and beloved brother
    c) my fellow prisoner
    d) son of comfort

Quiz 181

Two for Thessalonica

*This quiz covers both of Paul's letters to the Thessalonian
believers. See how well you can sort out these questions.*

1. Fill in the blank: "Even Jesus, which delivered us from the
_____ to come. . ."

2. Choose A or B: Paul sent Timothy to the believers at
Thessalonica, and Timothy brought back a A) good
report of their faith and charity B) report that they were
puffed up and should have been in mourning.

3. What description does Paul use to illustrate his gentleness toward those at Thessalonica?
   - a) a tender teacher, showing meekness to all people
   - b) as a hen gathers her chicks under her wings
   - c) as a lamb dumb before his shearer
   - d) as a nurse cherishes her children

4. When the Lord himself descends from heaven with a shout, who shall rise first?
   - a) the dead in Christ
   - b) the living believers
   - c) the prophets of the old law
   - d) those reserved for a terrible judgment

5. Fill in the blank: Paul says that the Lord will come as a "_____ in the night."

6. What two-word sentence does Paul state about rejoicing?

7. What three-word sentence does Paul state about praying?

8. What four-word sentence does Paul say about the Spirit?

9. Because some at Thessalonica were busybodies and disorderly, what command did Paul repeat that he had given them earlier about working and eating?

10. Paul told brethren at Thessalonica to be not weary in what?
    - a) admonishing the unbelievers
    - b) keeping the faith
    - c) waiting on the coming of the Lord
    - d) well doing

Quiz 182

Letter to a Young Pastor

Paul's first letter to Timothy is the focus of this quiz. What advice and counsel did he have for this young pastor?

1. Fill in the blank: "Now the end of the commandment is charity out of a pure heart, and of a good conscience, and of _____ unfeigned."

2. Paul writes that it is a faithful saying that Christ Jesus came into the world to do what?

3. In Paul's letter to Timothy, how does Paul say that a woman should adorn herself?
   - a) in a pattern of sincerity
   - b) with well-braided hair as a covering
   - c) covered from her head to her foot
   - d) with modest apparel

4. To which office does Paul say that by desiring it, a person desires a good work?
   - a) bishop
   - b) deacon
   - c) elder
   - d) preacher

5. Fill in the blank: "Now the Spirit speaketh expressly, that in the latter times some shall depart from the faith, giving heed to _____ spirits, and doctrines of devils."

6. How does Paul describe what has been done to the conscience of those who depart from the faith in the latter times?

7. What does Paul tell Timothy to "let no man despise"?

8. A person who does not care for his own, and especially for those of his own house, is worse than what?
      a) a man whose sin is open to the world
      b) a proud man, knowing nothing
      c) a publican
      d) an infidel

9. Fill in the blank: "But godliness with _____ is great gain."

10. What is the root of all evil?

Quiz 183

More Letters to Young Pastors

The questions in this quiz are based on 2 Timothy and Titus. How well do you recall the themes of these letters?

1. What are the names of Timothy's mother and grandmother?
      a) Anna and Pricilla
      b) Eunice and Lois
      c) Hermogenes and Claudia
      d) Susana and Joanna

2. Fill in the blank: "For God hath not given us the spirit of
_____; but of power."

3. Paul, who knows who he has believed, is persuaded that
He (God) is able to do what?

4. Paul told Timothy to study to show himself approved by
whom?

5. What type of speech did Paul tell Timothy to shun?

6. True or False: All Scripture is given by inspiration of God.

7. Fill in the blank: "I have fought a good fight, I have
finished my course, I have kept the _____."

8. In writing to Titus, when does Paul say the hope of
eternal life was promised by God?
    a) at the birth of Jesus
    b) at the resurrection of Jesus
    c) before the world began
    d) when Abraham offered Isaac

9. Who does Paul say the aged women should teach?
    a) children of the Cretians
    b) no one; they should be silent
    c) unbelieving husbands
    d) young women

10. Choose A or B: Although Paul says he was sometimes
foolish, disobedient, and living in malice, he was saved by
A) his works of righteousness B) the mercy of God.

Jesus in Hebrews

*The sacrifice of Jesus is a theme that runs throughout
the epistle to the Hebrews. This quiz should remind
you of the price He paid for our redemption.*

1. According to the writer of Hebrews, in "these last days"
   how does God speak to us?
   - a) by His Son
   - b) by the Holy Spirit
   - c) by the writings of all who are holy
   - d) by the fathers who work out salvation with fear
     and trembling

2. What does the writer of Hebrews say that Jesus had to
   "taste" for every man?

3. Why is Jesus able to succour [comfort, give relief] to those
   who are tempted?

4. The writer of Hebrews says that Jesus was tempted in all
   points, yet was without what?

5. True or False: The writer of Hebrews says that
   Melchisedec was made a priest like the Son of God
   because he served as a priest for a little while.

6. What do those believers do who have tasted the good
   word of God but then fall away?
   a) they bear reproach upon all believers
   b) they crucify the son of God afresh
   c) they fill the face of the world with hypocrisy
   d) their good memories perish

7. Rather than the blood of goats and calves, what did Christ
   take into the holy place?

8. How does the writer of Hebrews tell believers to run the
   race that is set before them?
   a) every man his own race
   b) to bring disciples the Word
   c) with patience
   d) without vanity

9. Fill in the blank: "Looking unto Jesus the author and
   _____ of our faith. . ."

10. Fill in the blanks: Jesus has said, "I will never _____
    thee, nor _____ thee."

Quiz 185

The Old Testament in Hebrews

The epistle to the Hebrews contains many references to the Old Testament. See how many of these references you can sort out in this quiz.

1. In times past how did God speak to the fathers?

2. Fill in the blank: "Thou madest him a little lower than the _____; thou crownedst him with glory and honour."

3. The writer of Hebrews says that the word of God is a discerner of what?
   a) a great people
   b) shouts of joy from weeping of the people
   c) the thoughts and intents of the heart
   d) what His servants taste and what they eat

4. Jesus is a priest forever after the order of who?
   a) Aaron   c) David
   b) Abraham   d) Melchisedec

5. What does the title of Melchisedec, "King of Salem," mean?

6. What does the writer of Hebrews say about the father and mother of Melchisedec?

7. True or False: The law made everything perfect.

8. Fill in the blank: "For if that first covenant had been _____, then should no place have been sought for the second."

9. What was one of the items after the second veil [Holiest of all] in the tabernacle?
    a) Aaron's rod that budded
    b) five golden emerods
    c) Moses' staff
    d) the serpent of brass

10. It is impossible for the blood of bulls and goats to do what?

Quiz 186

Faith's Hall of Fame

All the questions in this quiz are based on the eleventh chapter of Hebrews. How well do you remember these Old Testament people of faith?

1. Fill in the blanks: "Now faith is the _____ of things hoped for, the _____ of things not seen."

2. Choose A or B: The one who offered a more excellent sacrifice was A) Abel B) Cain.

3. Who built the city that Abraham looked for?

4. Who did not see death?
   a) Barak
   b) Enoch
   c) Jephathe
   d) Pharaoh's daughter

5. For God to keep his promise, what did Abraham think God would do after Abraham offered his son?

6. True or False: The parents of Moses hid him for three months because they were afraid of the king's command.

7. Fill in the blank: Moses chose to suffer "affliction with the people of God" rather than "to enjoy the _____ of sin for a season."

8. Who are the women mentioned by name in "faith's hall of fame" chapter in Hebrews?
   a) Rahab, Abigail, and Jochebed
   b) Eve and Sara
   c) Miriam
   d) Sara and Rahab

9. In speaking of the trials that the heroes of faith endured, what does the Hebrew writer say was not worthy of them?

10. What does the writer of Hebrews say about those who obtained a good report through faith?
   a) God provided something better for them.
   b) They received not the promise.
   c) They will carry a mark of those who grieve and repent.
   d) They will find sanctuary in New Jerusalem.

Quiz 187

Quotable Hebrews

*So you think you know Hebrews? Find out if you
do by supplying the missing words from some
of this book's most memorable passages.*

1. Fill in the blanks: "And, Thou, Lord, in the beginning hast laid the foundation of the earth; and the heavens are the works of _____ _____"

2. Fill in the blank: "Sit on my right hand, until I make thine enemies thy _____."

3. Fill in the blank: "How shall we escape, if we _____ so great salvation."

4. Fill in the blank: "But exhort one another daily, while it is called ____ ____; lest any of you be hardened through the deceitfulness of sin."

5. The writer of Hebrews says that the word of God is quick, and powerful, and sharper than what?
   - a) a critic's tongue
   - c) a flying arrow
   - b) a flint knife
   - d) a two-edged sword

6. Fill in the blank: "Ye have. . .become such as have need of _____, and not of strong meat."

7. Fill in the blank: "It is _____ unto men once to die, but after this the judgment."

8. Fill in the blank: "I will put my laws into their hearts, and in their minds will I write them; and their sins and iniquities will I _____ no more."

9. Fill in the blank: "Let us hold fast the profession of our faith without _____."

10. Some believers have entertained angels unawares when they entertained who?
    a) hard-to-please guests
    b) hungry relatives
    c) strangers
    d) traveling evangelists

Quiz 188

James on Faith

What does the epistle of James have to say about faith? Find out by answering these challenging questions.

1. The trying of a believer's faith worketh [develops] what?

2. What is it when a person knows to do good, but doesn't do it?

3. What does James say can save the sick?

4. After saying that believers should ask in faith without wavering, what else does James point out?
   - a) a double-minded man is unstable in all his ways
   - b) darkness and sorrow shall follow them
   - c) the Lord does not keep His promises to those who waver
   - d) the Lord reigns over those who stay the course

5. James says believers should not be hearers only of the word, but what?

6. After his discussion of unequal treatment of the rich and poor, James concludes by saying what?
   - a) "Be sorrowful, yet making many rich, even the poor."
   - b) "If ye have respect to persons, ye commit sin."
   - c) "Jesus, although rich, became poor for your sakes."
   - d) "The poor ye shall have with you always."

7. True or False: James says that the faith of a pure heart will warm and fill the poor and destitute.

8. Fill in the blank: "But wilt thou know, O _____ man, that faith without works is dead?"

9. Who does James use as examples of people who made faith perfect by works?
   - a) Abraham and Rahab
   - b) David and Samson
   - c) Ezekiel and Jeremiah
   - d) Noah and Jonah

10. Fill in the blanks: "For as the body without the spirit is _____, so faith without works is _____ also."

301

Quiz 189

Practically Speaking

*The epistle of James is known for its practical guidelines
for Christian living. Use these questions as
a measure of your own walk of faith.*

1. True or False: James says that when a person is tempted, he should say, "I am tempted of God."

2. What does sin bring forth when it is finished?

3. What phrase completes this quotation, "Every good gift and every perfect gift is from above, and cometh down from the Father of lights. . ."
   a) "who brings light to the shadow of death."
   b) "who gives light to the eye of the believer."
   c) "who guides ships in fierce winds."
   d) "with whom is no variableness, neither shadow of turning."

4. James tells believers to be slow to speak, slow to wrath, but swift to do what?
   a) guide others
   b) hear
   c) obey
   d) welcome the poor

5. What member of the body does James say is "an unruly evil, full of deadly poison"?

6. James says that those who ask, ask amiss, and do not receive it because they do what?
    a) ask for fire to consume the unbelievers
    b) seek another man's wealth
    c) consume it upon their lusts
    d) hide what they receive in the earth

7. Fill in the blank: "A friend of the world is the _____ of God."

8. If a believer resists the devil, what will the devil do?

9. In speaking of the rich, James compares the shortness of life to the flower of the grass, and in speaking of how a person cannot know what will happen tomorrow, James compares the shortness of life to what?

10. Fill in the blank: "The effectual fervent prayer of a righteous man availeth _____."

Quiz 190

Simon (Peter) Says. . .Part 1

These questions come from the first epistle of Peter.
How well do you recall Peter's teachings in this letter?

1. What phrase completes the statement beginning "be ye holy"?

2. According to Peter, believers will be born again to what kind of seed?
    a) fertile seed
    b) incorruptible seed
    c) seed of Isaac
    d) seed for the tree of knowledge of good and evil

3. To what type of vegetation does Peter compare all flesh?

4. Fill in the blank: "As newborn babes, desire the sincere _____ of the word."

5. What became of the stone that the builders disallowed?

6. Choose A or B: It is better for believers to suffer for A) well doing B) evil doing.

7. Although God resists the proud, what does He give to the humble?

8. To what does Peter compare baptism?
   a) a robe washed white
   b) eight souls saved by water
   c) Lot's wife and the pillar of salt
   d) sheep led by still water

9. Peter compares the devil to what roaring animal that seeks to devour?

10. At the end of this letter, how does Peter tell the believers to greet one another?
    a) with a "handshake of forbearance"
    b) with a "salute as heirs of salvation"
    c) with a "prayer and love feast"
    d) with a "kiss of charity"

Quiz 191

Simon (Peter) Says. . .Part 2

Peter's second epistle is the focus of these questions.
Consider this your second chance (Quiz 190 was your first)
to master the teachings of Peter.

1. Choose A or B: Peter compares one who knows righteousness but turns from it to a A) white sheep B) washed sow that becomes filthy again.

2. Fill in the blank: Peter says that in making the power of Jesus known, he did not follow "cunningly devised _____."

3. What statement from God does Peter say he heard when he was on the holy mountain with Jesus?

4. Who moved holy men of old time to speak prophecy?

5. What did God do to the angels that sinned?
    a) cast light upon them to show their wicked ways
    b) cast them down to hell
    c) changed them into brute beasts
    d) refined them with fire

6. Which person did Peter say was "vexed with the filthy conversation of the wicked"?
    a) Lot   c) Paul
    b) Noah   d) Peter himself

7. What does Paul say should be added to brotherly kindness?
    a) charity   c) knowledge
    b) godliness   d) temperance

8. What question will scoffers in the last days ask?

9. Fill in the blank: "The Lord is not _____ concerning his promise."

10. How does Peter say the "day of the Lord" will come?

Quiz 192

First John

*These questions are based on the first epistle of John.
See how well you do at recalling the major themes of this letter.*

1. John writes that the word of God and what else is not in people who say they have not sinned?

2. How can believers know that they know God?

3. Fill in the blanks: "But he that hateth his brother is in _____, and walketh in _____."

4. Fill in the blank: "Love not the world, neither the _____ that are in the world."

5. The lust of the flesh, lust of the eyes, and what else is of the world?

6. True or False: According to John, the Antichrist denies that Jesus is the Christ.

7. John's message is that from the beginning believers should do what?
   - a) be of the world
   - b) destroy false teachers
   - c) love one another
   - d) manifest mastery of the word of God

8. Why does John say that "he that loveth not knoweth not God"?

9. John says to not love in word, neither in tongue, but how?
   a) as stronger vessels
   b) in deed and in truth
   c) in pain and sorrow
   d) with hearts that condemn sin

10. What three persons or things bear witness in heaven?
   a) Abraham, Isaac, Jacob
   b) devils, angels, prophets
   c) Father, Word, Holy Ghost
   d) Spirit, water, blood

Quiz 193

Two More by John

Both 2 John and 3 John contain only one chapter each, but don't overlook them. You'll find some important teachings from each of these books in this quiz.

1. Fill in the blank: John addresses his second letter to the _____ lady.

2. What commandment does John say believers had from the beginning?

3. True or False: Deceivers should be bidden "God speed" after being turned away from a believer's house.

4. What did deceivers claim about Jesus?
     a) He did not come in the flesh.
     b) He was the prince of the air.
     c) His resurrection was spiritual rather than physical.
     d) Salvation through Him came only by circumcision.

5. John had many other things to tell the lady; how did he plan on doing so?
     a) He would bring it by the Holy Spirit.
     b) He would send it by Gaius.
     c) He would speak face to face.
     d) He would write it in a later letter.

6. How does John describe Gaius?
     a) fellow worker in chains
     b) friend to strangers
     c) man of well report
     d) well beloved

7. True or False: John wishes for Gaius to prosper and enjoy good health.

8. What brings John great joy?

9. What flaw did Diotrephes have?
     a) He refused to read John's letter.
     b) He loved to have preeminence.
     c) He would not accept being rebuked.
     d) He would not release his slaves.

10. Fill in the blank: "He that doeth good is of _____."

Don't Forget Philemon and Jude

You thought we had forgotten Philemon, didn't you? Wrong. We placed it here with Jude just to throw you off—and also because each of these books is just a few verses long. Have fun sorting them out!

1. In the opening to the letter to Philemon, how does Paul describe his own circumstances?
    a) a prisoner of Jesus Christ
    b) a servant of Jesus Christ
    c) an apostle without portfolio
    d) an elder of the elect church

2. Who does Paul say is "now profitable" to "thee [Philemon] and to me"?

3. Fill in the blank: "Perhaps he therefore departed for a _____, that thou shouldest receive him for ever."

4. Michael, the archangel, disputed with the devil about the body of whom?
    a) Abraham   c) Moses
    b) Lazarus   d) Stephen

5. Enoch is described as what number in descent from Adam?

6. True or False: Paul states that the entire letter to
   Philemon was written for him by another person.

7. Near the end of the letter, what did Paul ask Philemon to do?
   a) prepare a lodging for him
   b) send books and parchments that had been
      entrusted to him
   c) send warm clothing before winter
   d) write to Jerusalem and tell them about Paul's need
      for prayer

8. True or False: Jude is a letter written to Jude by Paul.

9. Fill in the blank: "Ye should earnestly _____ for the faith."

10. Who was it that "kept not their first estate"?

Quiz 195

The Revelation

*Congratulations! You've finally reached the last book of
the Bible. Let's celebrate by focusing in this quiz on just
one chapter from Revelation—chapter 1. This should
prepare you for the final lap of the race as you work your
way through Revelation in the next five quizzes.*

1. The Son of man had the keys of what?

2. Choose A or B: The words of the prophecy are to be
A) heard and kept because the time is at hand B) shut up
and sealed because the time is not yet.

3. Where were the seven churches located?
   a) Asia   c) Rome
   b) Mesopotamia   d) Spain

4. Who is "the faithful witness and the first begotten of the
dead"?

5. Where was John when he received the Revelation?
   a) the isle of Tarshish   c) the isle of Patmos
   b) the isle of Melita   d) the isle unto Paphos

6. Fill in the blanks: "I am Alpha and _____, the first and
the _____."

7. Which church is missing from this list of the seven churches:
Ephesus, Smyrna, Pergamos, Thyatira, Sardis, Laodicea?

8. In the vision of the one like the Son of man, what came
out of the mouth?

9. True or False: Revelation specifically states that the
person to whom God gave the vision was John.

10. In the vision, the seven stars are angels and the seven
candlesticks are what?
    a) seven brides   c) seven men of honest
                                 report
    b) seven churches   d) seven doors

Quiz 196

Seven Churches

Seven churches with strange names in just two chapters—
chapters 2 and 3 of Revelation—is the challenge you face in
this quiz. But you can handle it. On your mark, get set, go!

1. What did the church of Ephesus who tried "them which say
   they are apostles, and are not" find the false apostles to be?

   a) circumspect   c) liars

   b) dead spiritually   d) wicked workers

2. What tree is in the midst of the paradise of God that he
   who overcomes will be given to eat?

3. Fill in the blank: "I know the blasphemy of them which say
   they are Jews, and are not, but are the synagogue of _____."

4. If the church at Smyrna is faithful until death, Jesus will
   give them what kind of crown?

5. What will be written on the white stone that Jesus gives to
   him that overcometh?

   a) a message to prepare the way of the Lord

   b) a new name

   c) MENE, MENE, TEKEL, UPHARSIN

   d) a new commandment

6. Who was "that woman" whom the church at Thyatira
   suffered [tolerated]?

7. Choose A or B: To the church at Philadelphia, Jesus says, "Behold, I come A) quickly B) reluctantly."

8. Why did Jesus say He would spew the church of Laodicea out of His mouth?

9. Jesus says that the Laodiceans were wretched, and miserable, and poor, and blind, and naked; but what did the Laodiceans say?
   a) "I am rich."
   b) "I am true and righteous."
   c) "I love God."
   d) "I pray and fast daily."

10. What must a person open for Jesus to "come in to him, and will sup with him, and he with me."

Quiz 197

Pictures in Heaven

It's time to focus on all those strange beings for which Revelation is famous. You deserve extra credit if you get all these correct!

1. How many elders were seated around the throne in heaven?

2. True or False: The mighty angel that held a little book had his right foot on the sea and his left foot on a cloud.

3. What phrase describes the rider on the white horse?
    a) had a pair of balances in his hand
    b) his name was Death, and hell followed with him
    c) take peace from the earth
    d) went forth conquering, and to conquer

4. What color of horse is missing from this list: white, red, pale?

5. When the third angel blew a trumpet, what was the name of the star that fell upon the rivers and upon the fountains of the waters?
    a) Gopher wood   c) Shittim wood
    b) Sagittarius   d) Wormwood

6. The locusts that came out of the smoke of the pit had tails like what stinging animal?
    a) bees   c) scorpions
    b) fiery ants   d) serpents

7. Fill in the blanks: "Thou art worthy, O Lord, to receive glory and honour and power: for thou hast _____ all things, and for thy pleasure they are and were _____."

8. The mighty angel said that when John ate the book it would taste how in his mouth?

9. Fill in the blanks: "And there was war in heaven: Michael and his _____ fought against the dragon; and the dragon fought and his _____."

10. What is the number that is "the number of the beast: for it is the number of a man"?

Quiz 198

Pictures of Heaven

Most believers wonder what heaven will be like. This quiz is a good overview of Revelation's teachings on the subject.

1. Fill in the blanks: "The _____ of this world are become the _____ of our Lord, and of his Christ; and he shall reign for ever and ever."

2. Choose A or B; The phrase that describes the song that was sung before the throne is A) a new song B) a song of the ages.

3. John saw the holy city, New Jerusalem, coming down from God out of heaven, prepared in what way?

4. What names were written on the gates of the city?
    a) the names of the twelve wells of water inside the gates
    b) the twelve apostles
    c) the twelve tribes of the children of Israel
    d) the twelve princes that bear record in heaven

5. How many gates were in each of the four walls of New Jerusalem?

6. The gates of New Jerusalem were made of what precious substance?

7. True or False: John saw a temple in New Jerusalem.

8. What phrase describes the gold that appears in the streets of New Jerusalem?
    a) "as it were transparent glass"
    b) "gold beaten pure and without dross"
    c) "gold of idols melted in His ferment heat"
    d) "the gold of that place is good"

9. The leaves from the tree on either side of the river that came from the throne of God were used for what purpose?
    a) a shadow over the heads of the weary
    b) to be scattered to the whirlwind
    c) to show that harvest is near
    d) healing of the nations

10. Fill in the blanks: "And the Spirit and the bride say, _____. And let him that heareth say, _____. And let him that is athirst _____. And whosoever will, let him take the water of life freely."

Quiz 199

Death and Destruction

In addition to telling us about heaven (see Quiz 198),
Revelation also has a lot to say about death and resurrection.
This quiz focuses on these realities.

1. Fill in the blank: Those who had a victory over the beast sang the song of _____ the servant of God, and the song of the Lamb.

2. The seven angels came out of the temple with seven plagues, and one of the beasts gave them seven golden vials full of what?
   a) blood shed for the saints   b) deadly poison
   c) incense   d) the wrath of God

3. Armageddon is a word in what tongue, or language?

4. What was the woman sitting upon that was scarlet in color, was full of names of blasphemy, and had seven heads and ten horns?
   a) a beast   c) a dragon
   b) a bull   d) a pale horse

5. Babylon is called the mother of what?

6. The names Faithful and True, King of Kings, Lord of Lords, and The Word of God all apply to One who was sitting on a horse of what color?

7. What do the ten horns represent?

8. Fill in the blank: "Babylon the great is fallen, is fallen, and is become the habitation of _____."

9. Why do the merchants of the earth and shipmasters weep and mourn over the fall of Babylon?

10. What do the seven heads of the beast represent?
   - a) seven lying spirits
   - b) seven mountains
   - c) seven plagues
   - d) seven years until destruction comes

Quiz 200

The End of Time

What better way to conclude these quizzes than by focusing on last things as presented in the book of Revelation? Hope you enjoyed your trip through the Bible. And don't let this be the end of your learning about God's Word!

1. What was the angel going to do with the key and a great chain?

2. What was written on the twelve foundations of the wall of the great city that descended out of heaven?

3. Fill in the blanks: "And I saw a new heaven and a new
_____: for the first heaven and the first _____ were
passed away; and there was no more sea."

4. What phrase describes the lake into which the devil will
be cast?
   a) "a dry lake filled with whirlwinds"
   b) "dark waters covered with thick, black clouds"
   c) "of fire and brimstone"
   d) "transparent as glass"

5. True or False: The length of the city was twice the
breadth, and the height was twice the length.

6. Why did the city have no need of the sun or the moon?

7. What grew beside the river that came from the throne of God?
   a) a tree that could not be moved
   b) the tree of knowledge of good and evil
   c) the tree of life
   d) a tree that bare fruit once every one thousand years

8. True or False: John was told to seal the prophecies of this
book.

9. In Revelation, Jesus is said to be what kind of star?
   a) a star in the east   c) a star that shall arise in
                                    believers' hearts
   b) a star out of Jacob   d) the bright and morning star

10. What would happen to any person who took away from
the words of the book of this prophecy?

The 2,001st Question

So you've been through two thousand Bible trivia questions, covering every book from Genesis to Revelation. Now, let's make that knowledge practical, with the 2,001st question:

How can a person stay pure?

Answer:

By obeying [God's] word.
(Psalm 119:9 NLT)

Answer Key

1) Creation
1. "In the beginning" (Gen. 1:1)
2. form (Gen. 1:2)
3. "Let" (Gen. 1:3)
4. d) months (Gen. 1:14)
5. true (Gen. 1:20)
6. kind, kind (Gen. 1:25)
7. d) "in our image" (Gen. 1:26)
8. a) seed-bearing herbs and fruit (Gen. 1:29)
9. six (Gen. 1:31)
10. "very good" (Gen. 1:31)

2) Adam, Eve, and Eden
1. b) the dust of the ground (Gen. 2:7)
2. breath of life (Gen. 2:7)
3. garden (Gen. 2:8)
4. c) "to dress it and to keep it" (Gen. 2:15)
5. false (Gen. 2:10–14)
6. alone (Gen. 2:18)
7. name them (Gen. 2:19–20)
8. b) a rib (Gen. 2:21–22)
9. true (Gen. 2:23)
10. naked (Gen. 2:25)

3) The Fall
1. B) subtle, or subtil (Gen. 3:1)
2. their eyes were opened (Gen 3:7)
3. "Where art thou?" (Gen. 3:9)
4. d) all of the above (Gen. 3:14–15)
5. true (Gen. 3:16)
6. sweat (Gen. 3:19)
7. d) the mother of all living (Gen. 3:20)
8. true (Gen. 3:21)
9. A) they might eat of the tree of life and live forever (Gen. 3:22)
10. Cherubims and a flaming sword (Gen. 3:24)

4) Cain and Abel
1. false (Gen. 4:2)
2. "the fruit of the ground" (Gen. 4:3)
3. "the firstlings of his flock" (Gen. 4:4)
4. true (Gen 4:4–5)
5. b) sin (Gen. 4:6–7)
6. slew (Gen. 4:8)

7. "Am I my brother's keeper?" (Gen. 4:9)
8. A) "a fugitive and a vagabond" (Gen. 4:12)
9. c) Nod (Gen. 4:16)
10. d) Seth (Gen. 4:25)

5) Long Live the Ancients
1. b) 930 (Gen. 5:5)
2. c) Enos (Gen. 5:6)
3. Enoch was Methuselah's father (Gen. 5:21)
4. He walked with God and God took him (Gen. 5:24)
5. b) Enoch (365 years) (Gen. 5:8, 23, 27)
6. Noah (Gen. 5:28–29)
7. A) Lamech (Gen. 5:31)
8. a) Noah's grandfather (Gen. 5:25, 28–29)
9. d) 500 (Gen. 5:32)
10. Shem, Ham, and Japheth (Gen. 5:32)

6) Noah and His Ark
1. a) spirit (Gen. 6:3)
2. evil (Gen. 6:5)
3. true (Gen. 6:6)
4. grace (Gen. 6:8)
5. corrupt, violence (Gen. 6:11)
6. c) gopher (Gen. 6:14)
7. one (Gen. 6:16)
8. b) three (Gen. 6:16)
9. "to keep them alive" (Gen. 6:19)
10. B) all (Gen. 6:22)

7) The Flood
1. c) seven pairs (Gen. 7:2)
2. forty days and forty nights (Gen. 7:4)
3. Noah, his wife, his three sons, and their wives (Gen. 7:7)
4. two by two (Gen. 7:9)
5. B) the Lord (Gen. 7:16)
6. raven (Gen. 8:6–7)
7. rest (Gen. 8:9)
8. d) an olive leaf (Gen. 8:11)
9. altar (Gen. 8:20)
10. a) curse (Gen. 8:21)

8) God's Promise to Noah
1. fruitful, multiply (Gen. 9:1)

2. dread (Gen. 9:2)
3. A) meat for (Gen. 9:3)
4. seed (Gen. 9:9)
5. A) remember (Gen. 9:15)
6. a rainbow (Gen. 9:13)
7. true (Gen. 9:15)
8. everlasting (Gen. 9:16)
9. Ham (Gen. 9:18)
10. true (Gen. 9:19)

9) The Post-Flood World
1. Ham (Gen. 10:6–8)
2. A) hunter (Gen. 10:9)
3. a) Babel (Gen. 10:10)
4. language, speech (Gen. 11:1)
5. heaven (Gen. 11:4)
6. true (Gen. 11:5)
7. imagined (Gen. 11:6)
8. true (Gen. 11:7–8)
9. they stopped building it (Gen. 11:8)
10. c) Babel (Gen. 11:9)

10) Abram and Sarai
1. country (Gen. 12:1)
2. d) all of the above (Gen. 12:2–3)
3. Lot (Gen. 12:5)
4. Canaan (Gen. 12:5)
5. c) famine (Gen. 12:10)
6. A) sister (Gen. 12:13)
7. false; He plagued Pharaoh (Gen. 12:17)
8. d) (Gen. 17:5)
9. circumcised (Gen. 17:10)
10. Sarah (Gen. 17:15)

11) Two Sons for Abraham
1. Sarai's (Gen. 16:1–2)
2. true (Gen. 16:6-7)
3. The angel of the Lord (Gen. 16:9)
4. d) the angel of the Lord (Gen. 16:11)
5. "Thou God seest me" (Gen. 16:13)
6. b) archer (Gen. 21:14, 20)
7. a) 100 (Gen. 21:5)
8. Sarah (Gen. 21:6)
9. heir (Gen. 21:10)
10. A) grievous (Gen. 21:11)

12) Lot
1. cattle, silver, gold (Gen. 13:2)
2. B) strife (Gen. 13:7)
3. Abram (Gen. 13:8–9)
4. Jordan (Gen. 13:11)
5. the land of Canaan (Gen. 13:12)
6. wicked, sinners (Gen. 13:13)
7. b) Abram (Gen. 13:14–15)
8. d) Lot (Gen. 14:5, 12)
9. Salem (Gen. 14:18)
10. false (Gen. 14:22–23)

13) Sodom and Gomorrah
1. grievous (Gen. 18:20)
2. false; it was Abraham who pleaded for Sodom (Gen. 18:27, 32)
3. two (Gen. 19:1)
4. the people of Sodom (Gen. 19:4–5)
5. true (Gen. 19:9)
6. A) blindness (Gen. 19:11)
7. they did not believe him (Gen. 19:14)
8. b) Zoar (Gen. 19:22)
9. c) she looked back at the destruction of the city (Gen. 19:24–26)
10. his two daughters (Gen. 19:30)

14) Isaac
1. she laughed (Gen. 18:12)
2. false; it was his son Isaac (Gen. 22:1–2)
3. He indicated that God would provide a sacrificial lamb (Gen. 22:8)
4. slay (Gen. 22:10)
5. the angel of the Lord (Gen. 22:11)
6. a ram (Gen. 22:13)

7. b) the stars of heaven and the sands of the seashore (Gen. 22:17)
8. his chief servant (Gen. 24:2–4)
9. d) Rebekah (Gen. 24:15–19)
10. true (Gen. 24:58)

15) Jacob and Esau

1. false; Esau was Isaac's favorite, and Rebekah preferred Jacob
   (Gen. 25:28)
2. c) his birthright (Gen. 25:31–34)
3. Rebekah's (Gen. 27:6–10)
4. Esau was hairy and Jacob was smooth; he told the difference by touch
   (Gen. 27:11–12)
5. he wore Esau's clothes and put goat skins on his hands and neck
   (Gen. 27:15–16)
6. because his brother Esau threatened to kill him (Gen. 27:41–44)
7. true (Gen. 28:1–2)
8. B) a pillow (Gen. 28:11)
9. ladder (Gen. 28:12)
10. a) Bethel (Gen. 28:19)

16) Jacob's Strange Family, Part 1

1. Rachel (Gen. 29:10)
2. seven (Gen. 29:18)
3. Laban gave Jacob his daughter Leah instead of Rachel (Gen. 29:25)
4. B) Zilpah and Bilhah (Gen. 29:24, 29)
5. d) Reuben (Gen. 29:32)
6. Dinah (Gen. 30:21)
7. Leah (Gen. 30:20–21)
8. b) six (Gen. 30:19)
9. his images, or household gods (Gen. 31:19, 32)
10. c) Jacob (Gen. 31:43, 48–49)

17) Jacob's Strange Family, Part 2

1. B) wrestled (Gen. 32:24)
2. true (Gen. 33:2)
3. A) friendly (Gen. 33:4)
4. house (Gen. 33:17)
5. true (Gen. 34:2–4)
6. a) Simeon and Levi (Gen. 34:25–26)
7. altar (Gen. 35:1–7)
8. Israel (Gen. 35:10)
9. a) Benoni (Gen. 35:16–18)
10. false; she died while giving birth to Benjamin (Gen. 35:18–19)

18) Joseph
1. loved (Gen. 37:3)
2. B) many colors (Gen. 37:3)
3. seventeen (Gen. 37:2, 5)
4. c) sheaves of wheat (Gen. 37:7)
5. B) bowed (Gen. 37:9)
6. his father (Gen. 37:10)
7. coat, pit (Gen. 37:23–24)
8. b) Egypt (Gen. 37:28)
9. false; he was falsely accused by Potiphar's wife (Gen. 39:7–20)
10. d) he would be restored to his job (Gen. 40:2–13, 21)

19) Pharaoh's Dreams
1. b) two (Gen. 40:3; 41:1)
2. ate (Gen. 41:4)
3. seven good and seven thin ears of corn (Gen. 41:5–6)
4. true (Gen. 41:7–8)
5. Pharaoh's chief butler (Gen. 41:9–13)
6. seven years of plenty would be followed by seven years of famine
   (Gen. 41:29–30)
7. B) "discreet and wise" (Gen. 41:33)
8. ring (Gen. 41:42)
9. ruler (Gen. 41:43)
10. a) storing food (Gen. 41:46–49)

20) Israel in Egypt
1. to buy corn (Gen. 42:2)
2. d) mischief, or trouble, might befall him (Gen. 42:4)
3. governor (Gen. 42:6)
4. false; he knew them, but they didn't recognize him (Gen. 42:8)
5. spies (Gen. 42:14)
6. d) a silver cup (Gen. 44:2)
7. Judah (Gen. 44:18, 33)
8. true (Gen. 45:1–2)
9. Joseph (Gen. 50:19–20)
10. Joseph (Exod. 1:8)

21) Moses
1. because she couldn't hide him any longer (Exod. 2:3)
2. his sister (Exod. 2:4)
3. B) daughter (Exod. 2:5)
4. false; it was his mother (Exod. 2:7–8)
5. a) he was drawn out of the water (Exod. 2:10)

6. b) he killed an Egyptian man (Exod. 2:12, 15)
7. seven (Exod. 2:16)
8. his staff turned into a serpent; he put his hand in his robe and it became leprous and then he put it in his robe again and it returned to normal (Exod. 4:2–4, 6–7)
9. c) his brother Aaron (Exod. 4:14; 5:1)
10. true (Exod. 5:2)

22) The Plagues, Part 1
1. true (Exod. 7:10–12)
2. swallowed (Exod. 7:11–12)
3. water, blood (Exod. 7:20)
4. false; they also produced frogs (Exod. 8:6–7)
5. a) the finger of God (Exod. 8:19)
6. Goshen (Exod. 8:22)
7. hardened (Exod. 8:32)
8. d) serve (Exod. 9:1)
9. die (Exod. 9:4)
10. B) cattle (Exod. 9:6)

23) The Plagues, Part 2
1. a) ashes (Exod. 9:8)
2. true (Exod. 9:11)
3. false; he hardened his heart (Exod. 9:12)
4. A) stretch his rod toward heaven (Exod. 9:22–23)
5. true (Exod. 9:25)
6. Pharaoh (Exod. 9:27)
7. locusts (Exod. 10:4)
8. false; the locusts ate all the vegetation in the land (Exod. 10:15)
9. c) three (Exod. 10:23)
10. death of all the Egyptian firstborn (Exod. 11:5)

24) The Passover
1. A) male (Exod. 12:5)
2. blemish (Exod. 12:5)
3. c) fourteenth (Exod. 12:6)
4. true (Exod. 12:7)
5. unleavened, bitter (Exod. 12:8)
6. true (Exod. 12:11)
7. God said, "When I see the blood, I will pass over you, and the plague shall not be upon you to destroy you" (Exod. 12:13)
8. A) memorial (Exod. 12:14)
9. false; it was to last seven days (Exod. 12:15)
10. b) hyssop (Exod. 12:22)

25) The Exodus

1. jewels of silver, jewels of gold, and raiment (Exod. 12:35)
2. d) 430 (Exod. 12:40)
3. sanctify (Exod. 13:1–2)
4. c) It was at war (Exod. 13:17)
5. Joseph's bones (Exod. 13:19)
6. cloud, fire (Exod. 13:21)
7. his hand (Exod. 14:21)
8. dry (Exod. 14:22)
9. a) He took off their chariot wheels (Exod. 14:25)
10. one (Exod. 14:28)

26) Miracle Food and Drink

1. bread (Exod. 16:4)
2. false; they had to gather twice as much (Exod. 16:5)
3. c) quail (Exod. 16:13)
4. it spoiled and bred worms (Exod. 16:20)
5. B) people (Exod. 16:31)
6. rested (Exod. 16:30)
7. c) Sin (Exod. 17:1)
8. because they had no water to drink (Exod. 17:2)
9. true (Exod. 17:6)
10. false; he named it Massah and Meribah (Exod. 17:7)

27) The Ten Commandments

1. no other gods (Exod. 20:3)
2. c) graven image (Exod. 20:4)
3. A) the Lord is a jealous God (Exod. 20:5)
4. in vain (Exod. 20:7)
5. Remember (Exod. 20:8)
6. true (Exod. 20:12)
7. kill (Exod. 20:13)
8. adultery (Exod. 20:14)
9. false witness (Exod. 20:16)
10. d) all of the above (Exod. 20:17)

28) The Ark of the Covenant

1. c) shittim (Exod. 25:10)
2. false; the dimensions were two and a half cubits long, one and a half cubits wide, and one and a half cubits high (Exod. 25:10)
3. gold (Exod. 25:11)
4. to hold the staves used to carry the ark (Exod. 25:12–14)
5. the mercy seat (Exod. 25:17)

6. B) cherubim (Exod. 25:18)
7. B) wings (Exod. 25:20)
8. true (Exod. 25:22)
9. two tables, or tablets, of stone (Deut. 10:1–2)
10. c) Levi (Deut. 10:8)

29) The Tabernacle
1. ten (Exod. 26:1)
2. d) all of the above (Exod. 26:1)
3. vail, or veil (Exod. 26:33)
4. the ark of the testimony, or covenant (Exod. 26:34)
5. B) horns (Exod. 27:2)
6. brass (Exod. 27:2)
7. false; it was to be pure olive oil (Exod. 27:20)
8. a) twelve (Exod. 28:21)
9. true (Exod. 28:36)
10. b) Bezaleel (Exod. 31:1–7)

30) Golden Trouble
1. B) Moses was away a long time (Exod. 32:1)
2. up on the mountain (Exod. 32:1)
3. their gold earrings (Exod. 32:2)
4. Aaron (Exod. 32:2–4)
5. corrupted (Exod. 32:7)
6. B) break the stone tables, or tablets (Exod. 32:19)
7. true (Exod. 32:20)
8. B) Aaron cast the gold into the fire and it came out a calf (Exod. 32:24)
9. c) Levi (Exod. 32:26)
10. c) three thousand (Exod. 32:28)

31) Laws of Leviticus
1. burnt (Lev. 1:4)
2. d) priest offering (Lev. 3:1, 4:3, 6:6)
3. B) fat, of ox, or of sheep, or of goat (Lev. 7:23)
4. oil (Lev. 8:12)
5. false; it was Nadab and Abihu (Lev. 10:1–2)
6. unclean (Lev. 11:8)
7. d) hares (Lev. 11:6)
8. the priest (Lev. 13:2)
9. c) seven (Lev. 13:4)
10. true (Lev. 13:59)

32) More Laws of Leviticus

1. the priest (Lev. 14:2)
2. true (Lev. 14:9)
3. d) all of the above (Lev. 14:12–13)
4. false; several cleansings and inspections were required before the house was declared hopelessly contaminated and then destroyed (Lev. 14:37–45)
5. scapegoat (Lev. 16:8)
6. A) on the day it was offered (Lev. 19:5–6)
7. holy (Lev. 20:7)
8. true (Lev. 21:1)
9. it was not accepted (Lev. 22:20)
10. b) Aaron and his sons (Lev. 24:5–9)

33) Celebrations

1. convocations (Lev. 23:2)
2. rest (Lev. 23:3)
3. c) Passover (Lev. 23:5)
4. A) the first and seventh days (Lev. 23:7–8)
5. sheaf (Lev. 23:10–11)
6. true (Lev. 23:14)
7. The poor were allowed to gather what was left behind after the harvest (Lev. 23:22)
8. false; it was observed on the tenth day of the seventh month (Lev. 23:27)
9. b) seven (Lev. 23:34)
10. d) seven (Lev. 23:41–43)

34) Exploring Canaan

1. search, land (Num. 13:1–2)
2. twelve, one from each tribe (Num. 13:4–15)
3. B) up into a mountain (Num. 13:17)
4. d) all of the above (Num. 13:18–19)
5. B) the south (Num. 13:22)
6. false; they found huge clusters of grapes that two men had to carry on a pole between them (Num. 13:23)
7. d) forty (Num. 13:25)
8. milk, honey (Num. 13:27)
9. Caleb (Num. 13:30)
10. They refused to move out and take the land (Num. 13:31)

35) Rebellion

1. displeased (Num. 11:1)
2. a) Moses (Num. 11:11, 14)
3. God struck them with a plague (Num. 11:33)

4. c) he married an Ethiopian woman (Num. 12:1)
5. true (Num. 12:10, 15)
6. Joshua and Caleb (Num. 14:6–8)
7. "Surely they shall not see the land which I sware unto their fathers" (Num. 14:23)
8. forty years (Num. 14:33)
9. Joshua and Caleb (Num. 14:38)
10. true (Num. 14:39)

36) Wilderness Wanderings
1. c) fringes (Num. 15:38–39)
2. 250 (Num. 16:1–2)
3. Moses (Num. 16:4–5)
4. false; he caused the earth to open up and swallow Korah (Num. 16:30–33)
5. A) He caused Aaron's rod to blossom (Num. 17:8)
6. true (Num. 20:8)
7. because Moses didn't believe the Lord (Num. 20:12)
8. d) Hor (Num. 20:23, 28)
9. d) fiery serpents (Num. 21:5–6)
10. serpent (Num. 21:9)

37) Balaam and Balak
1. true (Num. 22:2, 5–6)
2. d) a and b (Num. 22:7)
3. b) God (Num. 22:12)
4. the princes of the land (Num. 22:15–16)
5. A) great honor (Num. 22:17)
6. true (Num. 22:20)
7. c) the angel of the Lord (Num. 22:23)
8. false; it was his donkey (Num. 22:28)
9. three (Num. 24:10)
10. false (Num. 24:10)

38) The Parting Words of Moses, Part 1
1. A) stars of heaven (Deut. 1:10)
2. Got the people to choose rulers over themselves (Deut. 1:13)
3. true (Deut. 1:27)
4. c) Lot (Deut. 2:9)
5. Og (Deut. 3:3)
6. a) He loved their fathers (Deut. 4:37)
7. one (Deut. 6:4)
8. gods (Deut. 6:14)
9. B) righteousness (Deut. 6:25)
10. possess (Deut. 7:1)

39) The Parting Words of Moses, Part 2
1. d) all of the above (Deut. 10:12)
2. utterly (Deut. 12:2)
3. blood (Deut. 12:16)
4. c) put him to death (Deut. 13:3–5)
5. d) roebuck (Deut. 14:4–5, 7–8, 12)
6. true (Deut. 14:22)
7. release (Deut. 15:1–2)
8. a) six (Deut. 15:12)
9. A) gates (Deut. 16:18)
10. true (Deut. 19:3)

40) Moses' End
1. b) 120 years old (Deut. 34:7)
2. true (Deut. 31:2)
3. Joshua (Deut. 31:7)
4. the priests, the sons of Levi (Deut. 31:9)
5. cloud (Deut. 31:15)
6. the Lord (Deut. 31:16)
7. A) Nebo (Deut. 34:1)
8. d) all the land He had promised the Israelites (Deut. 34:1–4)
9. c) thirty (Deut. 34:8)
10. face, face (Deut. 34:10)

41) Say Hello to Joshua
1. wisdom (Deut. 34:9)
2. b) cross the Jordan River and enter the Promised Land (Josh. 1:1–2)
3. given (Josh. 1:3)
4. true (Josh. 1:6)
5. meditating on and doing all that was written in the book of law (Josh. 1:8)
6. strong, courage (Josh. 1:9)
7. B) officers (Josh. 1:10–11)
8. c) three (Josh. 1:11)
9. true (Josh. 1:12, 14)
10. d) listen to Joshua as they had listened to Moses (Josh. 1:17)

42) Crossing Jordan
1. two (Josh. 2:1)
2. c) Rahab's (Josh. 2:1)
3. B) scarlet thread (Josh. 2:18)
4. true (Josh. 2:24)
5. a) the ark of the covenant (Josh. 3:6)
6. one (Josh. 3:12)

7. true (Josh. 3:15–16)
8. Jordan (Josh. 4:3)
9. that the waters of the Jordan were cut off before the ark of the covenant (Josh. 4:7)
10. false; they stood in the middle of the Jordan River until all the people had crossed over (Josh. 4:10)

43) Jericho
1. b) the captain of the host of the Lord (Josh. 5:13–14)
2. true (Josh. 6:1)
3. given, hand (Josh. 6:2)
4. once (Josh. 6:3)
5. a) seven (Josh. 6:4)
6. shout with a loud shout (Josh. 6:5)
7. flat (Josh. 6:5)
8. true (Josh. 6:15)
9. Rahab (Josh. 6:17)
10. false; they were put in the treasury of the house of the Lord (Josh. 6:24)

44) Stealing Trouble
1. a) Achan (Josh. 7:1)
2. Joshua (Josh. 7:2)
3. A) three thousand (Josh. 7:4)
4. chased (Josh. 7:5)
5. d) b and c (Josh. 7:6)
6. the Lord showed him (Josh. 7:14, 18)
7. true (Josh. 7:21)
8. B) in the middle of the man's tent (Josh. 7:23)
9. Joshua (Josh. 7:25)
10. d) he was stoned and burned (Josh. 7:25)

45) Battling for Canaan
1. The Israelites acted defeated and got the men of Ai to chase them, leaving the city undefended (Josh. 8:15–17)
2. false; they did conquer Ai on the second attempt (Josh. 8:18–23)
3. an altar (Josh. 8:30)
4. true (Josh. 9:1–15)
5. true (Josh. 9:23)
6. b) the Amorites (Josh. 10:5, 13)
7. utterly (Josh. 10:40)
8. true (Josh. 11:1)
9. b) thirty-one (Josh. 12:24)
10. possessed (Josh. 13:1)

46) Here Come the Judges

1. true (Judg. 2:16)
2. B) Caleb's (Judg. 3:9)
3. A) Moab (Judg. 3:15)
4. false; he used an ox goad (Judg. 3:31)
5. a) Abimelech (Judg. 9:1–2)
6. true (Judg. 9:1)
7. c) the first thing that came out of his house to meet him (Judg. 11:30–31)
8. A) Bethlehem (Judg. 12:8)
9. false; he had forty sons (Judg. 12:13–14)
10. evil (Judg. 13:1)

47) A Mighty Strong Woman

1. a) Canaan (Judg. 4:2)
2. false; Sisera was the captain of Jabin's army (Judg. 4:2)
3. palm tree (Judg. 4:5)
4. true (Judg. 4:8)
5. a woman (Judg. 4:9)
6. a) Kenite (Judg. 4:11)
7. true (Judg. 4:17)
8. She covered him with a mantle and gave him milk to drink (Judg. 4:18–19)
9. false; she pounded a tent peg, or nail, into his head (Judg. 4:21)
10. Deborah and Barak (Judg. 5:1–2)

48) Gideon

1. true (Judg. 6:2)
2. A) grasshoppers (Judg. 6:5)
3. a) threshing wheat (Judg. 6:11)
4. the fleece would be wet and the ground around it would be dry (Judg. 6:37)
5. the fleece would be dry and the ground around it would be wet (Judg. 6:39)
6. too, many, water (Judg. 7:4)
7. d) three hundred (Judg. 7:7)
8. false; they used trumpets and lamps (Judg. 7:20)
9. "The sword of the LORD, and of Gideon" (Judg. 7:20)
10. true (Judg. 7:22)

49) Samson and Friends (and Enemies)

1. c) Manoah (Judg. 13:22–24)
2. B) a lion and honey (Judg. 14:8, 14)
3. foxes (Judg. 15:2, 4)

4. three (Judg. 16:15)
5. the length of his hair (Judg. 16:17)
6. B) lords of the Philistines (Judg. 16:18)
7. false; they blinded him and put him in prison (Judg. 16:21)
8. d) Gaza (Judg. 16:21)
9. brass (Judg. 16:21)
10. true (Judg. 16:30)

50) The Story of Ruth
1. A) mother-in-law (Ruth 1:8)
2. a) Moab (Ruth 1:4)
3. Ruth (Ruth 1:16)
4. a) Bethlehem (Ruth 1:19)
5. A) bitter (Ruth 1:20)
6. d) Boaz's field (Ruth 2:3)
7. B) sleeping at his feet (Ruth 3:7)
8. false; she had a family kinsman who was closer than Boaz (Ruth 3:12)
9. true (Ruth 4:16)
10. B) Obed (Ruth 4:17)

51) Introducing Samuel
1. B) drunk (1 Sam. 1:13–14)
2. true (1 Sam. 1: 4, 6)
3. c) she had asked the Lord for a son (1 Sam. 1:20)
4. c) as soon as he was weaned (1 Sam. 1:24–28)
5. B) did not know the Lord (1 Sam. 2:12)
6. favor (1 Sam. 2:26)
7. "Speak, LORD; for thy servant heareth" (1 Sam. 3:9)
8. B) shall not (1 Sam. 3:14)
9. feared (1 Sam. 3:15)
10. Eli (1 Sam. 3:18)

52) Philistine Trouble
1. Eli's sons (1 Sam. 4:4–5)
2. the Philistines (1 Sam. 4:7–8)
3. true (1 Sam. 4:11)
4. B) neck (1 Sam. 4:18)
5. Eli's daughter-in-law, Phinehas's wife (1 Sam. 4:19–22)
6. B) Dagon was face down in front of the ark (1 Sam. 5:3)
7. false; He struck them with sores, or emerods (1 Sam. 5:8–9)
8. c) seven (1 Sam. 6:1)
9. cart (1 Sam. 6:7–8)
10. b) Abinadab (1 Sam. 7:1)

53) Give Us a King!

1. false; they took bribes and perverted justice (1 Sam. 8:1, 3)
2. true (1 Sam. 8:7)
3. donkeys (1 Sam. 9:19–20)
4. d) Benjamin (1 Sam. 9:21)
5. Samuel (1 Sam. 10:1)
6. true (1 Sam. 10:10)
7. b) Mizpeh (1 Sam. 10:17, 24)
8. true (1 Sam. 10:25)
9. b) Ammonites (1 Sam. 11:1)
10. false; this happened at Gilgal (1 Sam. 11:15)

54) A King in Trouble

1. a) Samuel (1 Sam. 12:6, 13)
2. A) offered a burnt offering (1 Sam. 13:10–13)
3. true (1 Sam. 13:19–20)
4. his son Jonathan (1 Sam. 14:24, 27)
5. a) Agag (1 Sam. 15:8)
6. obey (1 Sam. 15:22)
7. Samuel (1 Sam. 15:22–23)
8. true (1 Sam. 15:26–27)
9. Samuel (1 Sam. 15:32–33)
10. repented, Saul (1 Sam. 15:35)

55) Hello, David

1. outward, heart (1 Sam. 16:7)
2. eight (1 Sam. 16:10–11)
3. the Spirit of the Lord (1 Sam. 16:13)
4. b) an evil spirit (1 Sam. 16:14)
5. true (1 Sam. 16:23)
6. B) Philistine (1 Sam. 17:4)
7. d) five (1 Sam. 17:40)
8. Goliath (1 Sam. 17:43)
9. Goliath's sword (1 Sam. 17:50–51)
10. B) Jerusalem (1 Sam. 17:54)

56) Maniacal Monarch

1. A) soul (1 Sam. 18:3)
2. true (1 Sam. 18:5)
3. B) women (1 Sam. 18:7–8)
4. javelin (1 Sam. 18:11)
5. d) because the Lord was with David (1 Sam. 18:12)
6. B) shooting arrows (1 Sam. 20:20)

7. Goliath's sword (1 Sam. 21:8–9)
8. a) robe (1 Sam. 24:4)
9. David (1 Sam. 26:11)
10. true (1 Sam. 27:1–3)

57) Saul's Final Mistake
1. B) he was afraid (1 Sam. 28:5, 7)
2. true (1 Sam. 28:14)
3. b) the Philistines (1 Sam. 31:2)
4. B) an arrow (1 Sam. 31:3)
5. He fell upon a sword and took his own life (1 Sam. 31:4)
6. true (1 Sam. 31:5)
7. false; they mutilated his body and stripped off his armor
    (1 Sam. 31:8–9)
8. c) three (1 Sam. 31:8)
9. valiant (1 Sam. 31:12)
10. d) seven (1 Sam. 31:13)

58) King David
1. false; he condemned him and had him killed (2 Sam. 1:14–15)
2. b) Hebron (2 Sam. 2:3–4)
3. a) Abner (2 Sam. 2:8)
4. the elders of Israel (2 Sam. 5:3)
5. A) Uzzah (2 Sam. 6:6–7)
6. Saul (2 Sam. 6:20)
7. c) Nathan (2 Sam. 7:2)
8. B) Jonathan (2 Sam. 9:6)
9. true (2 Sam. 9:7, 13)
10. eat, king's, table (2 Sam. 9:13)

59) Royal Scandal
1. true (2 Sam. 11:2)
2. a) Hittite (2 Sam. 11:3)
3. false; David tried to trick Uriah into thinking the child had been
    fathered by him, Uriah (2 Sam. 11:8–9)
4. A) Joab (2 Sam. 11:14)
5. c) put at the front of the battle (2 Sam. 11:15)
6. he was killed in battle (2 Sam. 11:17)
7. Nathan the prophet (2 Sam. 12:1–4)
8. true (2 Sam. 12:14)
9. David (2 Sam. 12:19, 23)
10. d) Solomon (2 Sam. 12:24)

60) A Family Unravels
1. A) sister (2 Sam. 13:1)
2. false; her name was Tamar (2 Sam. 13:2)
3. he pretended to be sick (2 Sam. 13:6)
4. c) 2 years (2 Sam. 13:23, 28–29)
5. d) Geshur (2 Sam. 13:37)
6. Joab (2 Sam. 14:23)
7. praised, beauty (2 Sam. 14:25)
8. two years (2 Sam. 14:28)
9. false; he rebelled against David and declared himself king while David was still on the throne (2 Sam. 15:10–13)
10. true (2 Sam. 18:9, 14)

61) From David to Solomon
1. Absalom (1 Kings 1:5–6)
2. true (1 Kings 1:7)
3. Bathsheba (1 Kings 1:16–17)
4. Zadok, Nathan (1 Kings 1:34)
5. false; he grabbed the horns of the altar (1 Kings 1:50)
6. Solomon (1 Kings 1:52)
7. b) seven (1 Kings 2:11)
8. Bathsheba (1 Kings 2:13, 17)
9. true (1 Kings 2:24–25)
10. b) Joab (1 Kings 2:30–34)

62) Wisdom, Please
1. A) Pharaoh (1 Kings 3:1)
2. c) an aqueduct (1 Kings 3:1)
3. loved (1 Kings 3:3)
4. B) dream (1 Kings 3:5)
5. b) Gibeon (1 Kings 3:4–5)
6. true (1 Kings 3:7)
7. a) understanding (1 Kings 3:9)
8. A) pleased (1 Kings 3:10)
9. the custody of a child (1 Kings 3:22)
10. he ordered the child to be cut in half in order to determine the child's real mother (1 Kings 3:24–27)

63) Temple Builder
1. false; he was forbidden to build the temple (1 Kings 5:3)
2. Hiram (1 Kings 5:1–6)
3. they were floated on the sea (1 Kings 5:8–9)
4. wisdom (1 Kings 5:12)

5. A) narrow (1 Kings 6:4)
6. dwell, forsake (1 Kings 6:13)
7. gold (1 Kings 6:21)
8. B) cherubim (1 Kings 6:23)
9. c) flowers (1 Kings 7:32–36)
10. c) the priests (1 Kings 8:6)

64) Solomon's Glory
1. B) walk uprightly (1 Kings 9:4–5)
2. The Lord would cut off Israel (1 Kings 9:7)
3. d) all of the above (1 Kings 9:20–21)
4. three (1 Kings 9:25)
5. d) Sheba (1 Kings 10:1)
6. wisdom (1 Kings 10:4)
7. spices, precious, stones, gold (1 Kings 10:10–11)
8. true (1 Kings 10:14)
9. ivory (1 Kings 10:18)
10. b) twelve lions (1 Kings 10:20)

65) Wise and Foolish
1. loved (1 Kings 11:1)
2. true (1 Kings 11:2)
3. gods (1 Kings 11:2)
4. false; he had seven hundred wives and three hundred concubines
    (1 Kings 11:3)
5. B) evil (1 Kings 11:6)
6. true (1 Kings 11:7)
7. covenant, statutes, rend, kingdom (1 Kings 11:11)
8. a) Edom (1 Kings 11:14)
9. b) ten (1 Kings 11:31)
10. kill (1 Kings 11:40)

66) A Kingdom Divided
1. c) Shechem (1 Kings 12:1)
2. B) Egypt (1 Kings 12:2)
3. false; he rejected their counsel (1 Kings 12:8)
4. scorpions (1 Kings 12:14)
5. A) Judah (1 Kings 12:17)
6. He was stoned to death (1 Kings 12:18)
7. true (1 Kings 12:18)
8. Jeroboam (1 Kings 12:25, 28)
9. c) Bethel and Dan (1 Kings 12:29)
10. c) seventeen (1 Kings 14:21)

67) The Prophet Elijah

1. ravens (1 Kings 17:5–6)
2. true (1 Kings 17:10, 14)
3. true (1 Kings 17:22)
4. b) Carmel (1 Kings 18:19)
5. twelve (1 Kings 18:31)
6. false; it was four barrels (1 Kings 18:33)
7. water (1 Kings 18:38)
8. an angel (1 Kings 19:5–6)
9. d) seven thousand (1 Kings 19:18)
10. a) plowing (1 Kings 19:19)

68) Ahab and Jezebel

1. true (1 Kings 21:1, 3)
2. bread (1 Kings 21:4)
3. Jezebel (1 Kings 21:7)
4. false; she enlisted false witnesses to declare that Naboth had blasphemed
   God (1 Kings 21:10)
5. b) stoned (1 Kings 21:13)
6. Elijah (1 Kings 21:17–19)
7. because he didn't prophesy anything good about Ahab (1 Kings 22:8)
8. true (1 Kings 22:30)
9. c) Samaria (1 Kings 22:37)
10. blood (1 Kings 22:38)

69) The Prophet Elisha

1. whirlwind (2 Kings 2:11)
2. true (2 Kings 2:13–14)
3. A) bears (2 Kings 2:23–24)
4. false; he multiplied her oil (2 Kings 4:1–7)
5. Shunammite (2 Kings 4:35–36)
6. b) Syria (2 Kings 5:1)
7. true (2 Kings 5:10–12)
8. He was struck with Naaman's leprosy (2 Kings 5:22, 27)
9. b) an ax head (2 Kings 6:5–7)
10. chariots (2 Kings 6:17)

70) Royally Bad

1. evil (2 Kings 8:26–27)
2. Elisha (2 Kings 9:1–3)
3. A) smite the house of Ahab (2 Kings 9:7)
4. false; it was King Jehu who ordered her execution (2 Kings 9:30, 33)
5. departed not (2 Kings 14:24)

6. b) a month (2 Kings 15:13)
7. B) a captain of his army (2 Kings 15:23, 25)
8. true (2 Kings 15:29)
9. c) Shalmaneser, king of Assyria (2 Kings 17:1–3)
10. false; it was Hoshea (2 Kings 17:6–18)

71) Three Good Kings
1. Jehosheba (2 Kings 11:1–2)
2. seven years old (2 Kings 11:21)
3. false; the collection was for repairing the house of the Lord
   (2 Kings 12:4–5)
4. right (2 Kings 18:3)
5. true (2 Kings 18:4)
6. d) all of the above (2 Kings 18:5–6)
7. true (2 Kings 19:35–36)
8. b) eight years old (2 Kings 22:1)
9. A) the book of the law (2 Kings 22:8)
10. d) all of the above (2 Kings 23:3)

72) The End of the Line
1. c) Assyria (2 Kings 17:6)
2. heathen (2 Kings 17:8)
3. A) secretly (2 Kings 17:9)
4. d) the Lord their God (2 Kings 17:14, 16)
5. true (2 Kings 17:27–28)
6. a) Zedekiah (2 Kings 25:1–2)
7. Nebuchadnezzar (2 Kings 25:1)
8. d) all of the above (2 Kings 25:7)
9. true (2 Kings 25:8–9)
10. false; the poor were left in Judah to farm the land (2 Kings 25:12)

73) Temple Rebuilders
1. c) Cyrus (Ezra 1:1)
2. true (Ezra 1:5)
3. vessels (Ezra 1:7)
4. A) an altar (Ezra 3:3)
5. weakened, troubled (Ezra 4:4)
6. true (Ezra 4:11–12)
7. cease (Ezra 4:23)
8. d) Haggai and Zechariah (Ezra 5:1)
9. d) a and c (Ezra 5:2)
10. false (Ezra 6:1, 7)

74) Ezra the Priest
1. scribe (Ezra 7:6)
2. a) Artaxerxes (Ezra 7:6–7)
3. law (Ezra 7:10)
4. true (Ezra 7:11–13)
5. freely, offered (Ezra 7:15)
6. A) burnt offering (Ezra 8:35)
7. prayed (Ezra 10:1)
8. c) they wept (Ezra 10:1)
9. true (Ezra 10:6)
10. d) pleasure (Ezra 10:11)

75) Introducing Nehemiah
1. d) all of the above (Neh. 1:3)
2. B) cupbearer (Neh. 1:11)
3. false; Artaxerxes was the king (Neh. 2:1)
4. true (Neh. 2:6)
5. forest, timber (Neh. 2:8)
6. A) captains and horsemen (Neh. 2:9)
7. false; he went at night so he could inspect them secretly (Neh. 2:12–15)
8. the rulers of Jerusalem (Neh. 2:16, 18)
9. despised (Neh. 2:19)
10. b) Geshem (Neh. 2:19–20)

76) Putting Up Walls
1. A) sheep gate (Neh. 3:1)
2. B) fish gate (Neh. 3:3)
3. true (Neh. 3:5)
4. B) valley gate (Neh. 3:13)
5. lower, higher (Neh. 4:13)
6. Nehemiah (Neh. 5:7)
7. true (Neh. 5:12)
8. false; he refused to meet with them (Neh. 6:2–3)
9. a) fifty-two days (Neh. 6:15)
10. a) Hanani and Hananiah (Neh. 7:2–3)

77) Call for a Queen
1. Vashti (Esther 1:9)
2. d) because she refused to appear before his guests (Esther 1:10–12)
3. the King of Persia (Esther 1:13–15)
4. true (Esther 1:17)
5. b) his servants (Esther 2:2–4)
6. false; it was Hadassah (Esther 2:7)

7. b) cousin (Esther 2:7)
8. women (Esther 2:8)
9. true (Esther 2:10)
10. loved (Esther 2:17)

78) Attempted Holocaust
1. above (Esther 3:1)
2. c) wouldn't bow down to him (Esther 3:5)
3. false; he was determined to destroy all the Jews in the kingdom (Esther 3:6)
4. true (Esther 4:11)
5. sceptre (Esther 5:2)
6. a banquet (Esther 5:4)
7. c) had saved the king's life (Esther 6:2)
8. true (Esther 6:11)
9. b) Esther (Esther 7:4–6)
10. A) hanged (Esther 8:7)

79) Job Under Attack
1. a) Satan (Job 1:9)
2. true (Job 1:17–19)
3. blessed (Job 1:21)
4. Satan (Job 2:7)
5. potsherd, ashes (Job 2:8)
6. d) Job's wife (Job 2:9)
7. sin (Job 2:10)
8. Eliphaz, Bildad, Zophar (Job 2:11)
9. d) all of the above (Job 2:12)
10. b) seven (Job 2:13)

80) Friends, So-Called
1. Job (Job 3:1)
2. false; Eliphaz did (Job 4:1)
3. Bildad (Job 8:1–2)
4. d) all of the above (Job 11:2, 5, 7)
5. Job (Job 13:15)
6. true (Job 18:2)
7. c) righteous (Job 32:1)
8. justified (Job 32:2)
9. A) the others were older than him (Job 32:4)
10. d) Elihu (Job 36:1)

81) God Breaks His Silence
1. a) a whirlwind (Job 38:1)
2. foundations (Job 38:4)
3. a) sang (Job 38:4, 7)
4. joy (Job 38:7)
5. wisdom (Job 39:26)
6. Job (Job 40:3-4)
7. b) righteous (Job 40:8)
8. hook (Job 41:1)
9. heaven (Job 41:11)
10. like (Job 41:33)

82) The Wrap on Job
1. thought (Job 42:2)
2. d) all of the above (Job 42:7)
3. true (Job 42:7)
4. pray for them (Job 42:8)
5. twice (Job 42:10)
6. d) all of the above (Job 42:11)
7. false; they gave him an earring of gold (Job 42:11)
8. latter, beginning (Job 42:12)
9. true (Job 42:13)
10. c) four (Job 42:16)

83) Everyone's Favorite Psalm
1. want (Ps. 23:1)
2. false (Ps. 23:2)
3. c) restores them (Ps. 23:3)
4. A) paths (Ps. 23:3)
5. valley, shadow, evil (Ps. 23:4)
6. true (Ps. 23:4)
7. d) a table (Ps. 23:5)
8. anointest (Ps. 23:5)
9. a) goodness and mercy (Ps. 23:6)
10. dwell (Ps. 23:6)

84) Psalms Fill-in-the-Blanks, Part 1
1. Blessed (Ps. 1:1)
2. excellent (Ps. 8:1)
3. b) fool (Ps. 14:1)
4. wise (Ps. 19:7)
5. light, salvation (Ps. 27:1)
6. instruct (Ps. 32:8)

7. c) desires, heart (Ps. 37:4)
8. know (Ps. 46:10)
9. clean, spirit (Ps. 51:10)
10. remember (Ps. 77:11)

85) Psalms Fill-in-the-Blanks, Part 2
1. d) dwelling place (Ps. 90:1)
2. refuge (Ps. 91:2)
3. gladness, singing (Ps. 100:2)
4. sing, sing (Ps. 101:1)
5. bless, bless (Ps.103:1)
6. preserve, preserve (Ps. 121:7)
7. heritage (Ps. 127:3)
8. a) known (Ps. 139:1)
9. good (Ps. 145:9)
10. praise (Ps. 150:6)

86) Psalm 119
1. true
2. Blessed (Ps. 119:1)
3. that he might not sin against God (Ps. 119:11)
4. a) word (Ps. 119:89)
5. love (Ps. 119:97)
6. lamp, light (Ps. 119:105)
7. A) an heritage (Ps. 119:111)
8. hiding (Ps. 119:114)
9. b) upright (Ps. 119:137)
10. A) an everlasting (Ps. 119:142)

87) More from the Psalms
1. c) heathen (Ps. 2:1)
2. Salvation (Ps. 3:8)
3. A) sacrifices (Ps. 4:5)
4. d) all of the above (Ps. 15:1–2)
5. glory (Ps. 19:1)
6. A) enemies (Ps. 25:2)
7. righteous (Ps. 37:25)
8. B) patiently (Ps. 40:1)
9. soul (Ps. 42:1)
10. d) soul, disquieted (Ps. 42:11)

88) And Yet More from the Psalms
1. B) snow (Ps. 51:7)
2. d) all of the above (Ps. 62:7)
3. early (Ps. 63:1)
4. A) honor (Ps. 66:2)
5. A) king (Ps. 72:1)
6. heart (Ps. 73:1)
7. true (Ps. 90:12)
8. Establish (Ps. 90:17)
9. A) good (Ps. 92:1)
10. a) violin (Ps. 150:3–5)

89) Proverbially Speaking, Part 1
1. true (Prov. 1:1)
2. A) fear (Prov. 1:7)
3. sinners (Prov. 1:10)
4. c) discretion (Prov. 2:11)
5. Trust, understanding (Prov. 3:5)
6. B) substance (Prov. 3:9)
7. c) wisdom (Prov. 3:13)
8. true (Prov. 3:33)
9. instruction (Prov. 4:1)
10. a) diligence, life (Prov. 4:23)

90) Proverbially Speaking, Part 2
1. A) ear (Prov. 5:1)
2. true (Prov. 5:3)
3. true (Prov. 5:5)
4. ant (Prov. 6:6)
5. d) a haughty heart (Prov. 6:16–19)
6. mother (Prov. 6:20)
7. burned (Prov. 6:27)
8. d) all of the above (Prov. 8:2–3)
9. A) silver (Prov. 8:10)
10. false; wisdom was set up from the beginning (Prov. 8:23)

91) Proverbially Speaking, Part 3
1. d) all of the above (Prov. 9:13)
2. wise (Prov. 10:1)
3. A) memory (Prov. 10:7)
4. true (Prov. 11:1)
5. counsel (Prov. 11:14)
6. B) knowledge (Prov. 12:1)

7. true (Prov. 12:8)
8. inheritance (Prov. 13:22)
9. b) soft, wrath (Prov. 15:1)
10. word (Prov. 15:23)

92) Proverbially Speaking, Part 4
1. destruction, fall (Prov. 16:18)
2. false; this proverb should read, "Better is a dry morsel..." (Prov. 17:1)
3. true (Prov. 17:9)
4. loveth (Prov. 17:17)
5. friendly (Prov. 18:24)
6. true (Prov. 20:11)
7. way (Prov. 22:6)
8. true (Prov. 27:5)
9. d) wicked (Prov. 28:1)
10. d) the way of bees in their hives (Prov. 30:18–19)

93) What a Woman!
1. c) rubies (Prov. 31:10)
2. A) trust (Prov. 31:11)
3. true (Prov. 31:12)
4. willingly (Prov. 31:13)
5. a) gives them meat (Prov. 31:15)
6. B) strength (Prov. 31:17)
7. hand (Prov. 31:20)
8. true (Prov. 31:22)
9. B) elders (Prov. 31:23)
10. rejoice (Prov. 31:25)

94) Ecclesiastes
1. true (Eccles. 1:1)
2. vanity (Eccles. 1:2)
3. true (Eccles. 2:4, 11)
4. false; there is a time to cast away stones and a time to gather stones together (Eccles. 3:5)
5. d) all of the above (Eccles. 4:9–11)
6. fools (Eccles. 5:4)
7. true (Eccles. 7:11)
8. dead flies (Eccles. 10:1)
9. false; it should read, "He that diggeth a pit..." (Eccles. 10:8)
10. b) to fear God and keep His commandments (Eccles. 12:13)

95) Ecclesiastes Fill-in-the-Blanks
1. Preacher (Eccles. 1:1)
2. season (Eccles. 3:1)
3. vow, vow (Eccles. 5:5)
4. b) ointment (Eccles. 7:1)
5. fools (Eccles. 7:9)
6. joyfully (Eccles. 9:9)
7. might (Eccles. 9:10)
8. a) bread (Eccles. 11:1)
9. Creator (Eccles. 12:1)
10. work (Eccles. 12:14)

96) A Love Song
1. b) wine (Song of Sol. 1:2)
2. gold, silver (Song of Sol. 1:11)
3. A) doves' (Song of Sol. 1:15)
4. thorns (Song of Sol. 2:2)
5. d) banner (Song of Sol. 2:4)
6. mine (Song of Sol. 2:16)
7. ravished (Song of Sol. 4:9)
8. true (Song of Sol. 4:12)
9. c) desire (Song of Sol. 7:10)
10. A) seal (Song of Sol. 8:6)

97) Introducing Isaiah
1. d) Zedekiah (Isa. 1:1)
2. b) reason (Isa. 1:18)
3. false; He was sitting upon a throne (Isa. 6:1)
4. A) seraphim (Isa. 6:2)
5. six (Isa. 6:2)
6. an angel (Isa. 6:3)
7. Isaiah (Isa. 6:5)
8. coal (Isa. 6:6–7)
9. send (Isa. 6:8)
10. "Here am I; send me" (Isa. 6:8)

98) Prophecies of the Christ
1. virgin (Isa. 7:14)
2. Immanuel (Isa. 7:14)
3. true (Isa. 7:16)
4. child (Isa. 9:6)
5. B) government (Isa. 9:6)
6. name (Isa. 9:6)

7. c) King of Nations (Isa. 9:6)
8. increase (Isa. 9:7)
9. b) David's (Isa. 9:7)
10. A) zeal (Isa. 9:7)

99) Quotable Isaiah—Fill-in-the-Blanks
1. scarlet (Isa. 1:18)
2. d) swords (Isa. 2:4)
3. lamb (Isa. 11:6)
4. child (Isa. 11:6)
5. wounded (Isa. 53:5)
6. a) stripes (Isa. 53:5)
7. sheep (Isa. 53:6)
8. Seek (Isa. 55:6)
9. thoughts, thoughts (Isa. 55:8)
10. heavens (Isa. 55:9)

100) Historical Isaiah
1. a) Assyria (Isa. 36:1)
2. true (Isa. 36:1)
3. A) Rabshakeh (Isa. 36:2)
4. c) Rabshakeh (Isa. 36:6)
5. A) Nineveh (Isa. 37:37)
6. The shadow on the sundial went back 10 degrees (Isa. 38:5, 8)
7. Isaiah (Isa. 38:21)
8. Hezekiah showed him all the treasures of his kingdom (Isa. 39:2)
9. Isaiah told Hezekiah that all of his treasures would one day be taken to Babylon (Isa. 39:5–6)
10. peace, truth (Isa. 39:8)

101) Jeremiah the Prophet
1. d) all of the above (Jer.1:1–3)
2. command, speak (Jer. 1:7)
3. A) girdle (Jer. 13:1)
4. a) hope (Jer. 17:13)
5. true (Jer. 18:6)
6. the pastors, or leaders, of Judah (Jer. 23:2)
7. false; he likened them to good and bad figs (Jer. 24:1–5)
8. B) Baruch (Jer. 36:4)
9. true (Jer. 36:23)
10. mire (Jer. 38:6)

102) Quotable Jeremiah
1. b) knew (Jer. 1:5)
2. direct (Jer. 10:23)
3. peace (Jer. 29:11)
4. heart (Jer. 29:13)
5. everlasting (Jer. 31:3)
6. great, mighty (Jer. 33:3)
7. break, pluck (Jer. 45:4)
8. a) dismayed, save (Jer. 46:27)
9. Cursed (Jer. 48:10)
10. widows (Jer. 49:11)

103) The Fall of Jerusalem
1. ninth (Jer. 39:1)
2. true (Jer. 39:3)
3. fled (Jer. 39:4)
4. d) Jericho (Jer. 39:5)
5. false; it was the king of Babylon (Jer. 39:6)
6. Nebuchadnezzar (Jer. 39:11–12)
7. c) Jeremiah (Jer. 39:11)
8. true (Jer. 42:10, 14)
9. the people of Judah who went to Egypt (Jer. 44:8)
10. captive (Jer. 52:27)

104) A Lament
1. solitary (Lam. 1:1)
2. captivity (Lam. 1:3)
3. d) all of the above (Lam. 1:4)
4. A) beauty (Lam. 1:6)
5. d) because she had sinned grievously against the Lord (Lam. 1:8)
6. anger (Lam. 2:1)
7. true (Lam. 2:7)
8. mercies (Lam. 3:22)
9. great (Lam. 3:23)
10. days, old (Lam. 5:21)

105) The Prophet Ezekiel
1. false; he was among the captives in Babylon, or Chaldea (Ezek. 1:1–3)
2. true (Ezek. 2:2)
3. rebellious (Ezek. 2:3)
4. A) tile (Ezek. 4:1)
5. b) 390 days (Ezek. 4:4–5)
6. true (Ezek. 6:2)

7. B) cherubim (Ezek. 10:1)
8. c) son of man (Ezek. 14:3)
9. true (Ezek. 18:4)
10. false; he was told not to mourn her death at all (Ezek. 24:16)

106) Strange Visions
1. b) whirlwind (Ezek. 1:4)
2. true (Ezek. 1:4–5)
3. a) a man (Ezek. 1:5)
4. four, four (Ezek. 1:6)
5. lightning (Ezek. 1:14)
6. true (Ezek. 1:16)
7. d) live (Ezek. 37:3)
8. false; they came together and were covered with flesh and sinews (Ezek. 37:7–8)
9. breath (Ezek. 37:8)
10. true (Ezek. 37:11)

107) Ezekiel on the End Times
1. c) Judah and Israel (Ezek. 37:16)
2. a) Gog (Ezek. 38:1–2)
3. Jacob, Israel (Ezek. 39:25)
4. b) a high mountain (Ezek. 40:2)
5. reed (Ezek. 40:3)
6. false; it was about the temple (Ezek. 41:1)
7. A) lots (Ezek. 45:1)
8. just, just, just (Ezek. 45:10)
9. true (Ezek. 47:1)
10. LORD, there (Ezek. 48:35)

108) Introducing Daniel
1. true (Dan. 1:7)
2. purposed (Dan. 1:8)
3. B) eunuchs (Dan. 1:11)
4. c) ten (Dan. 1:15)
5. knowledge, wisdom (Dan. 1:17)
6. d) all of the above (Dan. 2:2)
7. false; it was made of gold, silver, brass, iron, and clay (Dan. 2:32–33)
8. king, kings (Dan. 2:37)
9. true (Dan. 2:37–40)
10. chief (Dan. 2:48)

109) A Fiery Furnace

1. c) gold (Dan. 3:1)
2. worship (Dan. 3:5)
3. b) Chaldeans (Dan. 3:8–12)
4. Shadrach, Meshach, and Abednego (Dan. 3:16–17)
5. false; he ordered it heated seven times hotter than normal (Dan. 3:19)
6. b) mighty men (Dan. 3:20)
7. true (Dan. 3:22)
8. Nebuchadnezzar (Dan. 3:25)
9. Son, God (Dan. 3:25)
10. true (Dan. 3:29)

110) The Lion's Den

1. a) Darius (Dan. 6:1, 16)
2. B) presidents and princes (Dan. 6:4)
3. true (Dan. 6:5)
4. true (Dan. 6:7)
5. Medes, Persians (Dan. 6:8)
6. c) three (Dan. 6:10)
7. false; he did his best to keep Daniel from being thrown into the lion's den (Dan. 6:14)
8. the king (Dan. 6:16)
9. an angel (Dan. 6:22)
10. true (Dan. 6:24)

111) Daniel on the End Times

1. d) serpent (Dan. 7:4–6)
2. Ancient (Dan. 7:9)
3. everlasting (Dan. 7:13–14)
4. true (Dan. 7:24)
5. a) the angel Gabriel (Dan. 8:16)
6. false; it caused him to faint and get sick (Dan. 8:27)
7. B) Michael (Dan. 12:1)
8. seal (Dan. 12:4)
9. true (Dan. 12:7)
10. Blessed (Dan. 12:12)

112) Hosea's Sad Story

1. d) all of the above (Hos. 1:1)
2. B) Gomer (Hos. 1:2–3)
3. three (Hos. 1:4, 6, 8–9)
4. d) God (Hos. 1:4, 6, 8–9)
5. b) Loruhamah (Hos. 1:6)

6. false; the Lord told Hosea to take her back (Hos. 3:1–2)
7. true (Hos. 3:1)
8. Egypt (Hos. 11:1)
9. true (Hos. 14:4)
10. right (Hos. 14:9)

113) The Prophet Joel

1. false; it would be a day of darkness and gloom (Joel 2:1–2)
2. quake, tremble (Joel 2:10)
3. b) heart (Joel 2:13)
4. A) spirit (Joel 2:28)
5. prophesy (Joel 2:28)
6. a) dream dreams (Joel 2:28)
7. A) see visions (Joel 2:28)
8. delivered (Joel 2:32)
9. true (Joel 3:17)
10. B) strangers (Joel 3:17)

114) Amos and Obadiah

1. d) herdsman (Amos 1:1)
2. true (Amos 1:1)
3. d) Nineveh (Amos 1: 3, 9, 11)
4. agreed (Amos 3:3)
5. true (Amos 9:14)
6. Edom (Obad. 1)
7. heathen, despised (Obad. 2)
8. violence (Obad. 10)
9. false; it would consume the house of Esau (Obad. 18)
10. Lord's (Obad. 21)

115) Jonah's Tale

1. b) Nineveh (Jon. 1:1–2)
2. true (Jon. 1:3)
3. They cast lots (Jon. 1:5–7)
4. Jonah's (Jon. 1:12)
5. prepared (Jon. 1:17)
6. d) three days and three nights (Jon. 1:17)
7. It vomited him onto dry land (Jon. 2:10)
8. a) angry (Jon. 4:1)
9. Jonah (Jon. 4:3)
10. true (Jon. 4:5)

116) Micah's Ministry
1. c) Hezekiah (Mic. 1:1)
2. Samaria and Jerusalem (Mic. 1:1)
3. A) high (Mic. 1:3)
4. b) graven images (Mic. 1:7)
5. A) iniquity (Mic. 2:1)
6. established (Mic. 4:1)
7. true (Mic. 4:7)
8. d) Bethlehem, ruler (Mic. 5:2)
9. true (Mic. 6:3)
10. pardoneth (Mic. 7:18)

117) Nahum and Habakkuk
1. a) Nineveh (Nah. 1:1)
2. slow (Nah. 1:3)
3. B) trouble (Nah. 1:7)
4. A) commandment (Nah. 1:14)
5. a) the citizens of Nineveh (Nah. 1:1; 3:5)
6. c) Habakkuk (Hab. 1:2)
7. Chaldeans (Hab. 1:6)
8. faith (Hab. 2:4)
9. B) iniquity (Hab. 2:12)
10. hinds' (Hab. 3:19)

118) Zephaniah and Haggai
1. b) King Josiah (Zeph. 1:1)
2. wrath (Zeph. 1:15)
3. true (Zeph. 1:16)
4. B) light and treacherous (Zeph. 3:4)
5. singing (Zeph. 3:17)
6. false; he prophesied during the reign of King Darius (Hag. 1:1)
7. the people (Hag. 1:2)
8. latter, former (Hag. 2:9)
9. true (Hag. 2:21)
10. c) Zerubbabel (Hag. 2:23)

119) The Prophet Zechariah
1. d) Darius (Zech. 1:1)
2. Turn, turn (Zech. 1:3)
3. B) doings (Zech. 1:6)
4. horse (Zech. 1:8)
5. b) measuring line (Zech. 2:1)
6. BRANCH (Zech. 3:8)

7. false; they were like an adamant stone (Zech. 7:12)
8. B) fury (Zech. 8:2)
9. true (Zech. 14:9)
10. holiness (Zech. 14:21)

120) The Last Book of the Old Testament
1. a) Israel (Mal. 1:1)
2. false; he hated Esau and loved Jacob (Mal. 1:2–3)
3. polluted (Mal. 1:7)
4. true (Mal. 1:8)
5. messenger (Mal. 3:1)
6. B) suddenly (Mal. 3:1)
7. c) by failing to give their tithes and offerings (Mal. 3:8)
8. tithes (Mal. 3:10)
9. A) healing (Mal. 4:2)
10. a) Elijah (Mal. 4:5)

121) One Amazing Pregnancy
1. a) the angel Gabriel (Luke 1:26–31)
2. "a virgin" (Luke 1:27)
3. favor (Luke 1:30)
4. Joseph (Matt. 1:19, Luke 1:27)
5. c) privily (Matt. 1:19)
6. in a dream (Matt. 1:20)
7. d) Nazareth (Luke 1:26)
8. false (Luke 1:34)
9. Elisabeth (Luke 1:40, 56)
10. their sins (Matt. 1:21)

122) A Genealogy
1. David (Matt. 1:1)
2. Abraham (Matt. 1:1)
3. Adam (Luke 3:38)
4. c) fourteen (Matt. 1:17)
5. false (Matt 1:1–17; Luke 3:23–38)
6. b) Judah [Judas or Juda] (Matt. 1:3, Luke 3:26)
7. Urias [Uriah] (Matt. 1:6)
8. d) Ruth (Matt. 1:5)
9. true [as Noe] (Luke 3:36)
10. Seth (Luke 3:38)

123) Special Delivery
1. Augustus (Luke 2:1)
2. a) Bethlehem (Luke 2:4–5)
3. They were afraid (Luke 2:9)
4. a) an angel (Luke 2:10)
5. B) all people (Luke 2:10–11)
6. Moses (Luke 2:22)
7. c) in the temple at Jerusalem (Luke 2:25, 27, 36–37)
8. in a dream (Matt. 2:12)
9. Egypt (Matt. 2:14)
10. Death of Herod (Matt. 2:19–20)

124) The Boyhood of Christ
1. Every year at Passover (Luke 2:41)
2. c) twelve years old (Luke 2:42)
3. a day's journey (Luke 2:44)
4. three days (Luke 2:46)
5. b) they were astonished (Luke 2:47)
6. b) "I must be about my Father's business" (Luke 2:49)
7. Nazareth (Luke 2:51)
8. false (Luke 2:51)
9. in her heart (Luke 2:51)
10. God, man (Luke 2:52)

125) John the Baptist
1. d) Zacharias and Elisabeth (Luke 1:5, 63)
2. prepared (Luke 1:17)
3. B) none of his relatives (Luke 1:61)
4. He wrote it on a writing table (Luke 1:63)
5. c) unloose the shoes of Jesus (Mark 1:7)
6. heaven (Matt. 3:2)
7. B) wild honey (Matt. 3:4)
8. b) "O generation of vipers" (Matt. 3:7)
9. Herod's birthday (Matt. 14:6)
10. His disciples (Matt. 14:12)

126) Jesus' Ministry Begins
1. sin (John 1:29)
2. a dove (Mark 1:10)
3. thirty years of age (Luke 3:23)
4. d) "This is my beloved Son, in whom I am well pleased" (Matt. 3:17)
5. forty days and forty nights (Matt. 4:2)
6. when Jesus was hungry (Luke 4:2–3)

7. B) both Jesus and the Devil (Luke 4:8–10)
8. gospel (Mark 1:14)
9. d) "the Spirit of the Lord is upon me" (Luke 4:18)
10. d) were filled with wrath (Luke 4:28)

127) The Sermon on the Mount
1. "theirs is the kingdom of heaven" (Matt. 5:3)
2. "they shall inherit the earth" (Matt. 5:5)
3. d) they shall see God (Matt. 5:8)
4. B) fulfill them (Matt. 5:17)
5. love (Matt. 5:44)
6. b) do so in secret (Matt. 6:4)
7. heart (Matt. 6:21)
8. lilies of the field (Matt. 6:28–29)
9. B) narrow (Matt. 7:14)
10. d) as wolves in sheep's clothing (Matt. 7:15)

128) Be Healed! Part 1
1. four (Mark 2:3)
2. the press of people blocked the way (Mark 2:4)
3. c) scribes (Mark 2:6–7)
4. the elders of the Jews (Luke 7:3)
5. true (Luke 7:6)
6. authority (Luke 7:8)
7. false; He had not found so great a faith (Luke 7:9)
8. d) ruler of the synagogue (Mark 5:22)
9. b) lay hands on her (Mark 5:23)
10. they laughed Him to scorn (Mark 5:40)

129) Be Healed! Part 2
1. false; he could speak plainly (Mark 7:35)
2. "Who did sin, this man, or his parents?" (John 9:2)
3. light (John 9:5)
4. b) pool of Siloam (John 9:7)
5. b) "I believe, help thou mine unbelief" (Mark 9:24)
6. prayer, fasting (Mark 9:29)
7. "Is it lawful to heal on the Sabbath day?" (Luke 14:3)
8. d) stood afar off (Luke 17:12)
9. to show themselves to the priests (Luke 17:14)
10. one (Luke 17:15)

130) Parables of Jesus

1. d) Wise people do what He says (Matt. 7:24)
2. fowls devoured them (Matt. 13:4)
3. on stony places (Matt. 13:5–6)
4. B) His disciples alone (Matt. 13:10)
5. a) those that fell among thorns (Matt. 13:22)
6. c) at the harvest (Matt. 13:30)
7. all that he had (Matt. 13:46)
8. "Who is my neighbour?" (Luke 10:29)
9. Jericho (Luke 10:30)
10. false (Luke 10:35)

131) More Parables of Jesus

1. eat, drink, merry (Luke 12:19)
2. b) his soul would be required of him (Luke 12:20)
3. carried it on his shoulders (Luke 15:5)
4. d) one sinner who repents (Luke 15:10)
5. a famine (Luke 15:14)
6. swine (Luke 15:15)
7. his elder brother (Luke 15:25, 28)
8. B) fewest talents (Matt. 25:18)
9. c) those who trusted in their own righteousness (Luke 18:9)
10. false (Luke 18:13)

132) Jesus Says, "I Am"

1. "and lowly in heart" (Matt. 11:29)
2. "Thou art the Christ" (Mark 8:29)
3. b) "even unto the end of the world" (Matt. 28:20)
4. life (John 8:12)
5. "Before Abraham was, I am" (John 8:58)
6. d) all of the above (John 10:7, 10–11)
7. true (John 11:23–25)
8. one (John 14:6)
9. b) as the husbandman (John 15:1)
10. branches (John 15:5)

133) Miracles of Jesus

1. b) His mother (John 2:3–4)
2. to teach the people (Luke 5:3)
3. b) "Depart from me; for I am a sinful man" (Luke 5:8)
4. prophet (Luke 7:16)
5. sleeping in the boat (Mark 4:38)
6. "Peace, be still" (Mark 4:39)

7. winds (Matt. 8:27)
8. true (Mark 6:38)
9. b) Andrew (John 6:8–9)
10. twelve (John 6:13)

134) More Miracles of Jesus

1. Jesus walking on the sea (Matt. 14:25)
2. false; this time there are seven loaves and "a few" fish (Matt. 15:34)
3. in the mouth of a fish (Matt. 17:27)
4. Martha (John 11:1)
5. b) after two days (John 11:6)
6. die (John 11:16)
7. Jerusalem (John 11:18)
8. four days (John 11:39)
9. B) right (John 18:10)
10. b) an hundred and fifty and three (John 21:11)

135) Jesus Prays

1. bread (Matt. 6:11)
2. glory (Matt. 6:13)
3. Peter, James, and John (Mark 14:32–33)
4. three (Matt. 26:44)
5. c) "Nevertheless not what I will, but what thou wilt" (Mark 14:36)
6. d) sleeping (Mark 14:37)
7. false; He did pray to His Father (John 17:1–5)
8. B) keep them from the evil (John 17:15)
9. sent, sent (John 17:18)
10. d) one, as He and the Father are one (John 17:21–23)

136) Teachings of Jesus

1. d) Tyre and Sidon (Matt. 11:21–22)
2. pray for them (Luke 6:28)
3. d) because they will find rest for their souls (Matt. 11:29)
4. c) "do good to them which hate you" (Luke 6:27)
5. sinners (Luke 6:32–34)
6. false; "It shall be opened" (Luke 11:9–10)
7. bread, bread, bread (John 6:33–35)
8. loved, loved (John 15:9)
9. A) love (John 15:12)
10. lay down his life for his friends (John 15:13)

137) More Teachings of Jesus

1. false; it followed Jesus healing a man (Matt.12:24–25)
2. "As ye have done it unto one of the least of these my brethren, ye have done it unto me" (Matt. 25:37, 40)
3. "Love the Lord thy God with all thy heart, and with all thy soul, and with all thy mind, and with all thy strength" (Mark 12:30)
4. captives (Luke 4:18)
5. b) proclaimed upon the housetops (Luke 12:3)
6. a) Jesus (John 3:16)
7. because their deeds were evil (John 3:19)
8. Spirit, spirit (John 4:24)
9. fruit (John 15:8)
10. c) Do whatever He commands (John 15:14)

138) The Twelve Disciples

1. b) fisherman (Mark 1:16)
2. Cephas (John 1:42)
3. c) Peter (Matt. 4:18)
4. c) the sons of Zebedee (Mark 3:17)
5. John (John 21:20)
6. because Matthew was a publican, or tax collector (Luke 5:29–30)
7. "My LORD and my God" (John 20:28)
8. Judas Iscariot (John 12:4–6)
9. Simon Peter (John 18:10)
10. false; Peter, James, and John were present (Mark 9:2)

139) Jesus on Money

1. in heaven (Matt. 6:19–21)
2. b) He will hate the one and love the other (Matt. 6:24)
3. whole, world (Matt. 16:26)
4. the kingdom of God (Matt. 6:31, 33)
5. two (Mark 12:42)
6. d) They gave out of their abundance, but she gave all she had (Mark 12:44)
7. a house of prayer (Mark 11:17)
8. a) camel (Mark 10:25)
9. true (Luke 14:12–14)
10. sell everything he had and give it to the poor (Luke 18:22)

140) Jesus and the Pharisees

1. "They that be whole need not a physician, but they that are sick" (Matt. 9:12)
2. "The bridegroom is with them" (Matt. 9:15)
3. a) by asking a question about the baptism of John the Baptist

(Matt. 21:23, 25)
4. false; they perceived He was talking about them (Matt. 21:42, 45)
5. "Ye blind guides, which strain at a gnat, and swallow a camel"
   (Matt. 23:23–24)
6. a) to find an accusation against Him (Luke 6:7)
7. false; he ate in their house (Luke 7:36)
8. a) hypocrisy (Luke 12:1)
9. true (John 3:1)
10. because He healed him on the Sabbath day (John 9:14–16)

141) Plotting Against Jesus
1. winebibber (Matt. 11:19)
2. c) They sought a reason to accuse Him (Mark 3:2)
3. true (Luke 13:14)
4. equal (John 5:18)
5. entangle (Matt. 22:15)
6. false; they asked no more questions (Matt. 22:46)
7. b) "Why tempt ye me, ye hypocrites?" (Matt. 22:18)
8. they feared the people because of Jesus' popularity (Luke 22:2)
9. c) "What will ye give me, and I will deliver him unto you?" (Matt. 26:15)
10. A) glad (Mark 14:11)

142) The Last Supper
1. c) Peter and John (Luke 22:8)
2. a pitcher of water (Luke 22:10)
3. d) "Thou shalt never wash my feet"(John 13:8)
4. to give them an example, to show that they should do as He had done
   (John 13:15)
5. true (John 13:24–25)
6. body (Luke 22:19)
7. His blood (Matt. 26:28–29)
8. thrice, or three times (Matt. 26:34)
9. prison (Luke 22:33)
10. d) sang a hymn (Matt. 26:30)

143) Jesus' Arrest

1. false; He looked at Peter (Luke 22:61)
2. d) the transgressors (Luke 22:37)
3. Gethsemane (Matt. 26:36)
4. A) pass from Him (Mark 14:35)
5. weak (Matt. 26:41)
6. three (Matt. 26:44)
7. c) "This is your hour, and the power of darkness" (Luke 22:53)
8. c) They went backward, and fell to the ground (John 18:6)
9. his right ear (John 18:10)
10. sword, sword, sword (Matt. 26:52)

144) A Traitor's End

1. false; they each asked if it was them (Matt. 26:22)
2. with a kiss (Matt. 26:49)
3. thirty (Matt. 27:3)
4. blood (Matt 27:4)
5. It was not lawful because it was the price of blood (Matt. 27:6)
6. c) hanged himself (Matt. 27:5)
7. to bury strangers in (Matt. 27:7)
8. the field of blood (Matt. 27:8, Acts 1:19)
9. b) Jesus' resurrection (Acts 1:22)
10. d) Matthias (Acts 1:26)

145) Jesus' Trial

1. They did not want to defile themselves; this would have kept them from eating the Passover (John 18:28)
2. d) He objected to giving tribute to Caesar (Luke 23:2)
3. "It is not lawful for us to put any man to death" (John 18:31)
4. "What is truth?" (John 18:38)
5. false; He was from Galilee (Luke 23:5, 7)
6. Caesar (John 19:15)
7. c) the wife of Pilate (Matt. 27:17, 19)
8. a reed (Matt. 27:29)
9. c) "Hail, King of the Jews!" (Mark 15:18)
10. Some miracle (Luke 23:8)

146) The Crucifixion

1. Simon of Cyrene (Matt. 27:32)
2. the place of a skull (John 19:17)
3. a) "Father, forgive them; for they know not what they do" (Luke 23:34)
4. four (John 19:23)
5. "THE KING OF THE JEWS" (Mark 15:26)

6. false; one was on His right and the other on His left (Mark 15:27)
7. "My God, my God, why hast thou forsaken me?" (Matt. 27:46)
8. b) Mary, His mother (John 19:25–27)
9. a) Darkness was over all the land for three hours (Matt. 27:45)
10. vinegar (John 19:29)

147) Jesus' Death
1. save (Matt 27:49)
2. b) a sponge on a hyssop reed (Mark 15:36, John 19:29)
3. d) The veil of the temple was torn from top to bottom (Matt. 27:51)
4. false; they went into the holy city, Jerusalem (Matt. 27:53)
5. Truly (Matt. 27:54)
6. a) the earthquake (Matt. 27:54)
7. true (Mark 15:40–41)
8. so the bodies would not remain on the cross on the Sabbath day (John 19:31)
9. soldiers broke their legs (John 19:32)
10. pierced (John 19:37)

148) The Burial of Jesus
1. Mary Magdalene (Mark 15:40)
2. a) Joseph of Arimathaea (Mark 15:43)
3. the centurion (Mark 15:44)
4. false; it was Nicodemus (John 19:39)
5. c) in a clean linen cloth (Matt. 27:59)
6. deceiver (Matt. 27:63)
7. d) no one (Luke 23:53)
8. hewn out of rock (Matt. 27:60)
9. A huge stone was rolled against the door (Matt. 27:60)
10. false; he told the Pharisees to do it (Matt. 27:62, 65–66)

149) He Is Risen!
1. b) an angel (Matt. 28:2)
2. the first day of the week (Mark 16:2)
3. dead (Luke 24:5)
4. the "other disciple" (John 20:4)
5. the napkin that was about his head (John 20:7)
6. Mary Magdalene (Mark 16:9)
7. d) gave them money (Matt. 28:12)
8. two (Luke 24:13)
9. false; they did not know Him (Luke 24:16)
10. b) spend the night with them (Luke 24:29)

150) More on the Resurrection
1. c) for fear of the Jews (John 20:19)
2. "Peace be unto you" (John 20:19)
3. d) they were terrified (Luke 24:37)
4. broiled fish and honeycomb (Luke 24:42)
5. remission (Luke 24:47)
6. b) to be filled with power from the Holy Spirit (Luke 24:49)
7. false; He did show them (John 20:20)
8. Thomas (John 20:24)
9. eight (John 20:26)
10. seen (John 20:29)

151) The Ascension
1. Holy, Ghost (Acts 1:5)
2. three (John 21:15–17)
3. false; Jesus did not make such a promise (John 21:23)
4. power (Matt. 28:18)
5. "whatsoever I have commanded you" (Matt. 28:19–20)
6. a) Bethany (Luke 24:50)
7. forty (Acts 1:3)
8. b) 153 (John 21:11)
9. a) in a cloud (Acts 1:9)
10. to Jerusalem and into an upper room (Acts 1:12–13)

152) Pentecost
1. a rushing mighty wind (Acts 2:2)
2. c) They were Galilaeans (Acts 2:7)
3. "These men are full of new wine" (Acts 2:13)
4. Joel (Acts 2:16–17)
5. a) dream dreams (Acts 2:17)
6. wicked (Acts 2:22–23)
7. pricked (Acts 2:37)
8. false; he said "repent, and be baptized" (Acts 2:38)
9. three thousand (Acts 2:41)
10. d) the Lord (Acts 2:47)

153) The Church Grows
1. prayers (Acts 2:42)
2. false; they listened to his message (Acts 8:6)
3. five (Acts 4:4)
4. "the son of consolation" (Acts 4:36)
5. c) land (Acts 4:37)
6. c) Solomon's porch (Acts 5:12)

7. d) Samaria (Acts 8:5)
8. sold their possessions (Acts 2:45)
9. "Understandest thou what thou readest?" (Acts 8:30)
10. c) "He was led as a sheep to the slaughter" (Acts 8:32)

154) Martyrdom
1. Grecians and Hebrews (Acts 6:1)
2. tables (Acts 6:2)
3. b) "a man full of faith and of the Holy Ghost" (Acts 6:5)
4. false; he "did great wonders and miracles among the people" (Acts 6:8)
5. b) He spoke blasphemous words against Moses (Acts 6:11)
6. persecuted (Acts 7:52)
7. true (Acts 7:54)
8. a) "I see the. . .Son of man standing on the right hand of God"
    (Acts 7:56–57)
9. those stoning Stephen laid their clothes at Saul's feet (Acts 7:58)
10. "Lord, lay not this sin to their charge" (Acts 7:60)

155) Persecution of Christians
1. d) all of the above (Acts 4:27)
2. c) the temple (Acts 5:19–20)
3. God, men (Acts 5:29)
4. true (Acts 5:34, 39)
5. James, the brother of John (Acts 12:1–2)
6. Peter (Acts 12:3–4)
7. Saul (Acts 8:3)
8. The disciples let him down over the city wall in a basket (Acts 9:25)
9. c) let them alone (Acts 5:34, 38)
10. the apostles (Acts 8:1)

156) Conversion of Saul
1. slaughter (Acts 9:1)
2. b) Jerusalem (Acts 9:2)
3. "Who art thou, Lord?" (Acts 9:4–5)
4. false; the Lord sent Ananias to tell Saul what to do (Acts 9:6, 10–11)
5. three (Acts 9:9)
6. b) "Much evil he hath done to thy saints at Jerusalem" (Acts 9:13)
7. the Gentiles (Acts 9:15)
8. Brother (Acts 9:17)
9. a) preached Christ in the synagogues in Damascus (Acts 9:19–20)
10. kill him (Acts 9:23)

157) Peter the Leader
1. A) Pilate (Acts 3:13)
2. God's Son Jesus (Acts 3:25–26)
3. a) "by the name of Jesus Christ of Nazareth" (Acts 4:10)
4. the Italian band (Acts 10:1)
5. a) "A devout man, and one that. . .prayed to God" (Acts 10:2)
6. false; he sent men to summon Peter as the angel commanded (Acts 10:7–8)
7. "Rise, Peter; kill, and eat" (Acts 10:13)
8. common, unclean (Acts 10:14)
9. b) Peter (Acts 10:34)
10. be baptized (Acts 10:48)

158) Miracles of the Apostles
1. b) Peter (Acts 3:6)
2. praised God (Acts 3:8)
3. false; they could see the man had been healed (Acts 4:14, 16)
4. since birth, or more than forty years (Acts 4:22)
5. a) Aeneas, who had palsy (Acts 9:33–34)
6. He raised her from the dead (Acts 9:37, 40)
7. coats and garments (Acts 9:39)
8. He would be blind for a season (Acts 13:8, 11)
9. A) healed a lame man (Acts 14:10–11)
10. Paul (Acts 20:9)

159) Paul's First Missionary Journey
1. Sergius Paulus (Acts 13:7)
2. John Mark (Acts 13:13; 15:37–38)
3. b) "If ye have any word of exhortation for the people, say on" (Acts 13:15)
4. B) the second Psalm (Acts 13:33)
5. justified, justified (Acts 13:39)
6. c) He was the chief speaker (Acts 14:12)
7. c) to sacrifice to Paul and Barnabas because he thought they were gods (Acts 14:11–13)
8. suffered (Acts 14:16)
9. elders (Acts 14:23)
10. Gentiles (Acts 14:27)

160) The Jerusalem Council
1. keep the law of Moses (Acts 15:5)
2. Peter (Acts 15:7)
3. difference (Acts 15:8–9)
4. d) They declared the miracles and wonders that God had done among the Gentiles (Acts 15:12)
5. James (Acts 15:13, 20)
6. b) Judas and Silas (Acts 15:22)
7. false; they made no such commandment (Acts 15:24)
8. c) men who "hazarded their lives" for the name of Jesus (Acts 15:25, 26)
9. four (Acts 15:29)
10. B) rejoiced (Acts 15:31)

161) Paul's Second Missionary Journey
1. baptized (Acts 16:33)
2. a) the Holy Ghost (Acts 16:6)
3. b) Macedonia (Acts 16:9)
4. B) were upset (Acts 16:19–20)
5. purple dye or cloth (Acts 16:14)
6. Timotheus [Timothy] (Acts 16:1)
7. a) Berea (Acts 17:10–11)
8. TO THE UNKNOWN GOD (Acts 17:23)
9. being (Acts 17:28)
10. Aquila and Priscilla (Acts 18:2)

162) Paul's Third Missionary Journey
1. false; he was "mighty in the Scriptures" (Acts 18:24)
2. Holy, Ghost (Acts 19:2)
3. Paul (Acts 19:15)
4. c) silversmith (Acts 19:24)
5. a) Ephesus (Acts 19:28)
6. B) do nothing rashly (Acts 19:36)
7. wolves (Acts 20:29)
8. d) Paul's own hands (Acts 20:34)
9. Jesus, as quoted by Paul (Acts 20:35)
10. They would "see his face no more" (Acts 20:38)

163) Apostle on Trial
1. false; they made no such claim (Acts 21:24)
2. d) Greeks (Acts 21:28)
3. Hebrew (Acts 21:40)
4. Paul was a Roman citizen (Acts 22:25–29)
5. He had no charges to bring against Paul (Acts 25:27)
6. convenient (Acts 24:25)
7. d) the resurrection (Acts 23:6–7)
8. true (Acts 26:27)
9. persuadest (Acts 26:28)
10. b) If he had not appealed to Caesar (Acts 26:32)

164) Roman Non-Holiday
1. A) courteously (Acts 27:3)
2. Crete (Acts 27:12)
3. d) the tackling of the ship (Acts 27:19)
4. Caesar (Acts 27:23–24)
5. none (Acts 27:34, 44)
6. with kindness (Acts 28:2)
7. c) Paul was a murderer (Acts 28:4)
8. false; no harm was spoken of him (Acts 28:21)
9. Gentiles (Acts 28:28)
10. b) preaching while living in a hired house (Acts 28:30–31)

165) A Letter to Rome
1. d) His resurrection from the dead (Rom. 1:4)
2. ashamed (Rom. 1:16)
3. respect (Rom. 2:11)
4. b) "no, not one" (Rom. 3:10)
5. shed blood (Rom. 3:15)
6. the glory of God (Rom. 3:23)
7. a) A man is justified by faith (Rom. 3:28)
8. false; there is no transgression (Rom. 4:15)
9. patience (Rom. 5:3)
10. sinners (Rom. 5:8)

166) Dead or Alive
1. grace (Rom. 6:1)
2. false; His death (Rom. 6:3)
3. death (Rom. 6:23)
4. as long as he lives (Rom. 7:1)
5. the body of Christ (Rom. 7:4)
6. b) the inward man (Rom. 7:22)

7. a) the believer's spirit (Rom. 8:16)
8. B) not seen (Rom. 8:24)
9. good (Rom. 8:28)
10. c) "who can be against us?" (Rom. 8:31)

167) The Rest of Romans
1. the clay (Rom. 9:21)
2. a) by hearing (Rom. 10:17)
3. Benjamin (Rom. 11:1)
4. riches (Rom. 11:33)
5. a) as a living sacrifice (Rom. 12:1)
6. with good (Rom. 12:21)
7. true (Rom. 13:1, 7)
8. doubtful (Rom. 14:1)
9. c) Spain (Rom. 15:24, 28)
10. with an holy kiss (Rom. 16:16)

168) Letter to a Church in Trouble
1. foundation (1 Cor. 3:11)
2. d) foolishness (1 Cor 1:23)
3. b) crucified (1 Cor. 2:2)
4. milk (1 Cor. 3:2)
5. b) given the increase (1 Cor. 3:6)
6. "Is Christ divided?" (1 Cor. 1:12–13)
7. A) foolishness (1 Cor. 3:19)
8. Timotheus [Timothy] (1 Cor. 4:17)
9. world (1 Cor. 6:2)
10. Holy, Ghost (1 Cor. 6:19)

169) Paul on Marriage
1. "Let every man have his own wife" (1 Cor. 7:1–2)
2. "The husband hath not power of his own body" (1 Cor. 7:4)
3. burn (1 Cor. 7:9)
4. calling, called (1 Cor. 7:20)
5. b) be reconciled to her husband (1 Cor. 7:11)
6. c) "seek not to be loosed" (1 Cor. 7:27)
7. A) belong to the Lord (1 Cor. 7:32–33)
8. c) how she may please her husband (1 Cor. 7:34)
9. better (1 Cor. 7:38)
10. "only in the Lord" (1 Cor. 7:39)

170) Spiritual Gifts
1. b) ignorant (1 Cor. 12:1)
2. Spirit (1 Cor. 12:4)
3. body (1 Cor. 12:20)
4. nothing (1 Cor. 13:2)
5. child, child, child, child (1 Cor. 13:11)
6. false; all three abide, but charity is the greatest (1 Cor. 13:13)
7. A) edifies the church (1 Cor. 14:5)
8. a) five (1 Cor. 14:19)
9. to them that believe not (1 Cor. 14:22)
10. a) confusion (1 Cor. 14:33)

171) Our Resurrection
1. the Scriptures (1 Cor. 15:3–4)
2. Cephas [Peter] (1 Cor. 15:5)
3. false; he saw Jesus (1 Cor. 15:8)
4. vain, vain (1 Cor. 15:14)
5. b) "We are of all men most miserable" (1 Cor. 15:19)
6. a) death (1 Cor. 15:26)
7. good, manners (1 Cor. 15:33)
8. birds (1 Cor. 15:39)
9. a) flesh and blood (1 Cor. 15:50)
10. victory (1 Cor. 15:54)

172) Another Letter to Corinth
1. false; that they might know his love (2 Cor. 2:4)
2. d) Titus (2 Cor. 2:13; 8:23)
3. c) a minister of the spirit of the new testament (2 Cor. 3:6)
4. when they turn to Christ (2 Cor. 3:13–16)
5. B) temporal (2 Cor. 4:18)
6. repentance to salvation (2 Cor. 7:10)
7. c) the temple of God (2 Cor. 6:16)
8. sparingly, sparingly, bountifully, bountifully (2 Cor. 9:6)
9. a cheerful giver (2 Cor. 9:7)
10. witnesses (2 Cor. 13:1)

173) Paul Defends Himself
1. flesh, flesh (2 Cor. 10:3)
2. false (2 Cor. 10:4)
3. false (2 Cor. 12:14)
4. five (2 Cor. 11:24)
5. thrice [three times] (2 Cor. 11:25)
6. a night and a day (2 Cor. 11:25)

7. a thorn in the flesh (2 Cor. 12:7)
8. d) weakness (2 Cor. 12:9)
9. b) not burdensome (2 Cor. 12:14)
10. d) the simplicity that is in Christ (2 Cor. 11:3)

174) Corinthians Fill-in-the-Blanks
1. devices (2 Cor. 2:11)
2. hearts (2 Cor. 3:2)
3. liberty (2 Cor. 3:17)
4. d) earthen (2 Cor. 4:7)
5. distressed, despair (2 Cor. 4:8)
6. hands (2 Cor. 5:1)
7. faith, sight (2 Cor. 5:7)
8. time, salvation (2 Cor. 6:2)
9. creature (2 Cor. 5:17)
10. a) fightings, fears (2 Cor. 7:5)

175) Letter to the Galatians
1. b) Jesus Christ and God the Father (Gal. 1:1)
2. any who preach any other gospel (Gal. 1:8–9)
3. faith (Gal. 3:11)
4. B) by the faith of Jesus Christ (Gal. 2:16)
5. a) Abraham (Gal. 3:7)
6. false; he went into Arabia (Gal 1:17)
7. b) a schoolmaster (Gal. 3:24)
8. their own eyes (Gal. 4:15)
9. B) freewoman (Gal. 4:23)
10. fruit of the spirit (Gal. 5:22–23)

176) Galatians Fill-in-the-Blanks
1. c) evil (Gal. 1:3–4)
2. Christ, Christ (Gal. 2:20)
3. blessed (Gal. 3:8)
4. curse, curse (Gal. 3:13)
5. Christ, Christ (Gal. 3:27)
6. liberty, liberty (Gal. 5:13)
7. lust (Gal. 5:16)
8. Spirit, Spirit (Gal. 5:25)
9. b) burdens (Gal. 6:2)
10. reap, reap, reap (Gal. 6:7–8)

177) Hello Ephesus
1. blood (Eph. 1:7)
2. a) all things (Eph. 1:22)
3. mercy (Eph. 2:4)
4. a) "and that not of yourselves: it is the gift of God" (Eph. 2:8)
5. B) Gentiles (Eph. 2:11, 3:1)
6. b) separation of Jews and Gentiles (Eph. 2:12, 14)
7. one, one, one (Eph. 4:4)
8. some, some, some, some (Eph. 4:11)
9. by sunset (Eph. 4:26)
10. "to him that needeth" (Eph. 4:28)

178) Practical Christian Living
1. darkness (Eph. 5:11)
2. a) because the days are evil (Eph. 5:16)
3. b) the Spirit (Eph. 5:18)
4. His church (Eph. 5:23–25, 32)
5. Honor thy father and mother (Eph. 6:2)
6. false; there is no "respect of persons" (Eph. 6:9)
7. the devil (Eph. 6:11)
8. b) flesh and blood (Eph. 6:12)
9. c) righteousness (Eph. 6:14)
10. Spirit (Eph 6:17)

179) A Word to the Philippians
1. d) he rejoices (Phil. 1:18)
2. gain (Phil. 1:21)
3. better than themselves (Phil 2:3)
4. a servant (Phil. 2:7)
5. Hebrews (Phil. 3:5)
6. a) a Pharisee (Phil. 3:5)
7. d) passeth all understanding (Phil. 4:7)
8. "think on these things" (Phil. 4:8)
9. content (Phil. 4:11)
10. strengtheneth (Phil. 4:13)

180) Dear Colossians
1. the power of darkness (Col. 1:13)
2. B) invisible (Col. 1:15)
3. church (Col. 1:18)
4. c) through philosophy and vain deceit (Col. 2:8)
5. on things above (Col. 3:2)
6. with psalms, hymns, and spiritual songs (Col 3:16)

7. deed (Col. 3:17)
8. salt (Col. 4:6)
9. c) do not provoke them to anger (Col. 3:21)
10. a) beloved physician (Col. 4:14)

181) Two for Thessalonica
1. wrath (1 Thess. 1:10)
2. A) good report of their faith and charity (1 Thess. 3:6)
3. d) as a nurse cherishes her children (1 Thess. 2:7)
4. a) the dead in Christ (1 Thess. 4:16)
5. thief (1 Thess. 5:2)
6. Rejoice evermore (1 Thess. 5:16)
7. Pray without ceasing (1 Thess. 5:17)
8. Quench not the Spirit (1 Thess. 5:19)
9. "If any would not work, neither should he eat" (2 Thess. 3:10)
10. d) well doing (2 Thess. 3:13)

182) Letter to a Young Pastor
1. faith (1 Tim. 1:5)
2. save sinners (1 Tim. 1:15)
3. d) with modest apparel (1 Tim. 2:9)
4. a) bishop (1 Tim. 3:1)
5. seducing (1 Tim. 4:1)
6. seared with a hot iron (1 Tim. 4:2)
7. his youth (1 Tim. 4:12)
8. d) an infidel (1 Tim. 5:8)
9. contentment (1 Tim. 6:6)
10. the love of money (1 Tim. 6:10)

183) More Letters to Young Pastors
1. b) Eunice and Lois (2 Tim. 1:5)
2. fear (2 Tim. 1:7)
3. keep that which he has committed to Him (2 Tim. 1:12)
4. God (2 Tim 2:15)
5. profane and vain babblings (2 Tim. 2:16)
6. true (2 Tim. 3:16)
7. faith (2 Tim. 4:7)
8. c) before the world began (Titus 1:2)
9. d) young women (Titus 2:3–4)
10. B) the mercy of God (Titus 3:3–5)

184) Jesus in Hebrews
1. a) by His Son (Heb. 1:1–2)
2. death (Heb. 2:9)
3. because He Himself was tempted (Heb. 2:18)
4. sin (Heb. 4:15)
5. false; he was "a priest continually" (Heb. 7:1, 3)
6. b) they crucify the son of God afresh (Heb. 6:5–6)
7. His own blood (Heb. 9:12)
8. c) with patience (Heb. 12:1)
9. finisher (Heb. 12:2)
10. leave, forsake (Heb. 13:5)

185) The Old Testament in Hebrews
1. by the prophets (Heb. 1:1)
2. angels (Heb. 2:7)
3. c) the thoughts and intents of the heart (Heb. 4:12)
4. d) Melchisedec (Heb. 5:5–6)
5. "King of Peace" (Heb. 7:2)
6. "without father, without mother" (Heb. 7:3)
7. false; it made "nothing perfect" (Heb. 7:19)
8. faultless (Heb 8:7)
9. a) Aaron's rod that budded (Heb. 9:3–4)
10. take away sins (Heb. 10:4)

186) Faith's Hall of Fame
1. substance, evidence (Heb. 11:1)
2. A) Abel (Heb. 11:4)
3. God (Heb. 11:10)
4. b) Enoch (Heb. 11:5)
5. raise him from the dead (Heb. 11:19)
6. false; they were not afraid (Heb. 11:23)
7. pleasures (Heb. 11:25)
8. d) Sara and Rahab (Heb. 11:11, 31)
9. the world (Heb. 11:38)
10. b) They received not the promise (Heb. 11:39)

187) Quotable Hebrews
1. thine, hands (Heb. 1:10)
2. footstool (Heb. 1:13)
3. neglect (Heb. 2:3)
4. To, day (Heb. 3:13)
5. d) a two-edged sword (Heb. 4:12)
6. milk (Heb. 5:12)

7. appointed (Heb. 9:27)
8. remember (Heb. 10:16–17)
9. wavering (Heb. 10:23)
10. c) strangers (Heb. 13:2)

188) James on Faith
1. patience (James 1:3)
2. sin (James 4:17)
3. the prayer of faith (James 5:15)
4. a) "a double-minded man is unstable in all his ways" (James 1:8)
5. doers of the word (James 1:22)
6. b) "If ye have respect to persons ye commit sin" (James 2:9)
7. false; faith without works is dead (James 2:15–17)
8. vain (James 2:20)
9. a) Abraham and Rahab (James 2:21–22, 25)
10. dead (James 2:26)

189) Practically Speaking
1. false; God cannot tempt anyone (James 1:13)
2. death (James 1:15)
3. d) "with whom is no variableness, neither shadow of turning" (James 1:17)
4. b) hear (James 1:19)
5. the tongue (James 3:8)
6. c) consume it upon their lusts (James 4:3)
7. enemy (James 4:4)
8. flee (James 4:7)
9. a vapour (James 1:10; 4:14)
10. much (James 5:16)

190) Simon (Peter) Says. . .Part 1
1. "for I am holy" (1 Pet. 1:16)
2. b) incorruptible seed (1 Pet. 1:23)
3. grass (1 Pet. 1:24)
4. milk (1 Pet. 2:2)
5. it was made the head of the corner (1 Pet. 2:7)
6. A) well doing (1 Pet. 3:17)
7. grace (1 Pet. 5:5)
8. b) eight souls saved by water (1 Pet. 3:20–21)
9. lion (1 Pet. 5:8)
10. d) with a "kiss of charity" (1 Pet. 5:14)

191) Simon (Peter) Says. . .Part 2
1. B) washed sow (2 Pet. 2:22)
2. fables (2 Pet. 1:16)
3. "This is my beloved Son, in whom I am well pleased" (2 Pet. 1:17–18)
4. the Holy Ghost (2 Pet. 1:21)
5. b) cast them down to hell (2 Pet. 2:4)
6. a) Lot (2 Pet. 2:7)
7. a) charity (2 Pet. 1:7)
8. "Where is the promise of his coming?" (2 Pet. 3:3–4)
9. slack (2 Pet. 3:9)
10. as a "thief in the night" (2 Pet. 3:10)

192) First John
1. the truth (1 John 1:8)
2. by keeping His commandments (1 John 2:3)
3. darkness, darkness (1 John 2:11)
4. things (1 John 2:15)
5. the pride of life (1 John 2:16)
6. true (1 John 2:22)
7. c) love one another (1 John 3:11)
8. because God is love (1 John 4:8)
9. b) in deed and in truth (1 John 3:18)
10. c) Father, Word, Holy Ghost (1 John 5:7)

193) Two More by John
1. elect (2 John 1)
2. love one another (2 John 5)
3. false; he is not to be received or bidden "God speed" (2 John 10)
4. a) He did not come in the flesh (2 John 7)
5. c) he would speak face to face (2 John 12)
6. d) well-beloved (3 John 1)
7. true (3 John 2)
8. that his children walk in truth (3 John 4)
9. b) He loved to have preeminence (3 John 9)
10. God (3 John 11)

194) Don't Forget Philemon and Jude
1. a) a prisoner of Jesus Christ (Philem. 1)
2. Onesimus (Philem. 10–11)
3. season (Philem. 15)
4. c) Moses (Jude 9)
5. seventh (Jude 14)
6. false; he wrote it in his "own hand" (Philem. 19)

7. a) prepare a lodging for him (Philem. 22)
8. false (Jude 1)
9. contend (Jude 3)
10. angels (Jude 6)

195) The Revelation
1. of hell and of death (Rev 1:18)
2. A) heard and kept because the time is at hand (Rev. 1:3)
3. a) Asia (Rev. 1:4)
4. Jesus (Rev. 1:5)
5. c) the isle of Patmos (Rev. 1:9)
6. Omega, last (Rev. 1:11)
7. Philadelphia (Rev. 1:11)
8. a sharp, two-edged sword (Rev. 1:13, 16)
9. true (Rev. 1:1, 4)
10. b) seven churches (Rev. 1:20)

196) Seven Churches
1. c) liars (Rev. 2:2)
2. the tree of life (Rev. 2:7)
3. Satan (Rev. 2:9)
4. a crown of life (Rev. 2:10)
5. b) a new name (Rev. 2:17)
6. Jezebel (Rev. 2:20)
7. A) quickly (Rev. 3:7, 11)
8. they were lukewarm, neither hot nor cold (Rev. 3:14–16)
9. a) "I am rich" (Rev. 3:17)
10. the door (Rev. 3:20)

197) Pictures in Heaven
1. "four and twenty" (Rev. 4:4)
2. false; his left foot was on the earth (Rev. 10:2)
3. d) went forth conquering, and to conquer (Rev. 6:2)
4. black (Rev. 6:2–8)
5. d) Wormwood (Rev. 8:10–11)
6. c) scorpions (Rev. 9:7–10)
7. created, created (Rev. 4:11)
8. sweet as honey (Rev. 10: 9)
9. angels, angels (Rev. 12:7)
10. "Six hundred threescore and six" (Rev. 13:18)

198) Pictures of Heaven

1. kingdoms, kingdoms (Rev 11:15)
2. A) a new song (Rev. 14:3)
3. as a bride adorned for her husband (Rev. 21:2)
4. c) the twelve tribes of the children of Israel (Rev. 21:12)
5. three (Rev. 21:13)
6. pearl (Rev. 21:21)
7. false; God and the Lamb are the temple (Rev. 21:22)
8. a) as it were transparent glass (Rev. 21:21)
9. d) healing of the nations (Rev. 22:2)
10. Come, Come, come (Rev. 22:17)

199) Death and Destruction

1. Moses (Rev. 15:1–3)
2. d) the wrath of God (Rev. 15:7)
3. Hebrew (Rev. 16:16)
4. a) a beast (Rev. 17:3)
5. harlots (Rev. 17:5)
6. white (Rev. 19:11, 13, 16)
7. ten kings (Rev. 17:12)
8. devils (Rev. 18:2)
9. they were made rich by her (Rev. 18:2, 15, 19)
10. b) seven mountains (Rev. 17:9)

200) The End of Time

1. bind the dragon, the Devil (Rev. 20:1–2)
2. the names of the twelve apostles (Rev. 21:10, 14)
3. earth, earth (Rev. 21:1)
4. c) "of fire and brimstone" (Rev. 20:10)
5. false; all three were equal (Rev. 21:16)
6. the glory of God gave light and the Lamb is the light (Rev. 21:23)
7. c) the tree of life (Rev. 22:2)
8. false; "seal not the sayings" (Rev. 22:10)
9. d) the bright and morning star (Rev. 22:16)
10. God would take away his part out of the book of life (Rev. 22:19)

If you enjoyed

Bible Trivia Challenge,

be sure to read

The 365 Day Bible
Word Game Challenge

This collection of word
puzzles will keep readers
occupied for an entire year.
Each puzzle tests players'
biblical knowledge as well
as problem-solving ability.

ISBN 978-1-61626-963-0
384 pages